THE FIRST
120
DAYS

What a New College
President Must Do
To Succeed

JEROLD PANAS

INSTITUTIONS PRESS

JEROLD PANAS

is Executive Partner of one of the nation's premier consulting firms to higher education. He is a platform personality of note and the author of twelve books.

ALSO BY JEROLD PANAS

MEGA GIFTS
Who Gives Them, Who Gets Them

BORN TO RAISE
What Makes A Great Fundraiser;
What Makes A Fundraiser Great

FUNDRAISING ALMANAC
Facts, Figures, and Anecdotes

BOARDROOM VERITIES
A Celebration of Trusteeship with Some
Guides and Techniques to Govern By

EXCEL!

FINDERS KEEPERS
Lessons I've Learned About
Dynamic Fundraising

WIT, WISDOM & MOXIE
A Fundraiser's Compendium of Wrinkles,
Strategies, and Admonitions That Really Work

ASKING
A 59-Minute Guide to Everything Board Members,
Volunteers, and Staff Must Know to Secure the Gift

MAKING THE CASE
The No-Nonsense Guide to Writing the
Perfect Case Statement

IT'S A WONDERFUL LIFE

FUNDRAISING HABITS OF SUPREMELY SUCCESSFUL BOARDS
A 59-Minute Guide to Assuring
Your Organiation's Future

*Copies of this book or any of those listed above are available from
the publisher. Quantity orders will receive a discount.*

CONTENTS

1

THE HIGH PRIZE
(What Do You Do?)

It is Saturday, January 21. The year is 1961.

The time is precisely 8:52 in the morning. The grandfather clock in the Oval Office will soon strike nine o'clock.

It is his first day in the White House. The new president walks over to an absolutely clean desk. Not a paper in sight. By his side is his Press Secretary, Pierre Salinger.

John F. Kennedy settles slowly in his chair. He looks at his spotless desk, then turns to his Press Secretary and says: "Okay, Pierre. What do I do now?"

You, as a new president of a college*, can identify with that. That's the question that gnaws. "What do I do now?" It's your most piercing challenge.

---

* In this book, I refer to all my institutions as "colleges." Actually, among smaller private colleges nationally, about two out of five now carry the title "university" in their name. For some, it may seem a stretch of sorts. It appears, however, the number is growing steadily. Among all institutions of higher education, the number using the title "university" is about 60 percent.

What you do in the early months of your tenure is critical. The first 120 days you are in office can determine the success of your presidency. Or…well, let's face it— your failure. "Sometimes you're the windshield, and sometimes you're the bug," goes a country song.

To test the importance of the first 120 days, I interviewed over fifty college and university presidents. It's a varied group as you will discover, and a wonderful mix. You will, by the way, be hearing from many of these presidents throughout these pages.

They all agree on one point. They all agree! Emphatically! The first 120 days sets the course for the new president.

So what do you do when you stand at the crossroads and there isn't a signpost in sight? It can be a daunting time, those first 120 days. Daunting . . . and exhilarating. I'll give you a roadmap for the journey. And some clear directions on how to get to your successful destination.

When you were selected to be president, the board said in effect— now it's up to you. "We'll help, but if you ever had dreams of leadership and a presidency, now is the time. This is the place. And you are the one we have chosen. We need you."

You touch the future. You are now a college president. You have drawn a high prize in the lottery of life.

Like President Kennedy, you find your way to your new office (it's not always ready for you and I'll discuss that later), you settle into your chair, and look at your clean desk. All of a sudden, everything explodes.

You become frantically busy dealing with faculty problems, student complaints, telephone calls from the board chair, finding a parking space, rushing to the next meeting, dealing with senior staff issues, trying to balance the budget, speaking to the freshman class, talking with a concerned parent, sending off a letter that's already late, looking over for the third time the 27 phone calls you have to return, and attending a practice session of the women's volleyball team.

And that's only the first day! It won't get any better.

You remember the White Queen's admonition to Alice. "It takes all the running you can do to just keep in the same place. If you want to get somewhere else, you must run twice as fast as that."

You really have no time to think about tomorrow, let alone the long-term future. It can be an unnerving, perplexing, series of unending and growing frustrations. You wonder where the time goes. The day is ending and you haven't even had time to look at your To Do list.

There will be times you see yourself stationary, fixed in place. Yet moving. It is like standing still on one of those long moving walkways at an airport. Eventually, you are deposited at the end.

C.J. Prahalad and Gary Hamel, in their seminal, *Competing for the Future*, estimate that the president spends less than three percent of his time in the first 120 days considering the long term future and strategic planning for the college. You will find there simply isn't time to think and plan.

Everyone is watching and taking note. The faculty, board members, senior administrative staff, students, even the maintenance staff— everyone.

The behavior of a new president sometimes spreads like a virus. Early accidents can alienate the college community, turn off financial supporters, and undermine her credibility. Everyone is looking for clues.

You learn by listening to others on the campus. But you must become quickly involved in shaping events rather than having them shape you. You must be vital and imaginative. You make things happen. You don't let things happen to you.

But here's the rub. You don't have the luxury of time to settle in. Probably no more than 120 days. Action is eloquence and admired, writes Shakespeare. Your action during those early months are so critical to your success.

For one thing, the men and women on the Selection Committee who chose you did so because they feel you are the perfect person for the position. They believe you will add value and needed strength to the college. The quicker they see you gaining in decisiveness and momentum, the greater their comfort and confidence.

There's something else. Everyone is keeping an eye on how you establish the style of your leadership. Your spirit and fervor. Key members of your team will take cues about their own involvement and work habits from the urgency and priorities you demonstrate. You ignite the spark.

Everyone is measuring you. The entire campus. These are the times in life it is important to understand the difference between the ropes to skip and the ropes to know.

In the first 120 days of your tenure, you must strain to establish your parameters. Those initial impressions can easily become self-fulfilling prophecies. Sadly so.

Once impressions harden, there is very little the new president can do in the short term to alter them. That is why it is so vitally important in those early days to think carefully about all your actions, your meetings, and your speeches. The college community is testing your mettle.

Every day, in front of hundreds, you have to do the *salto mortale*. That's circus parlance for an aerial double somersault performed on the tightrope without a net. In those first 120 days, you don't have a net.

Those first 120 days! No other time will a president be under such intense scrutiny and at the same time have such dramatic influence on the perceptions of others. You must do your very best and think carefully about all you do. It's what Thomas Jefferson had in mind in his first days of the presidency when he spoke of, "the splendid unending misery."

The Selection Committee chose you because they were seeking the very best for their particular situation. And you, you above everyone else, were their choice.

The Committee feels you add important value to the college. In addition, they believe there are some characteristics and skills that are sorely needed and that you bring those in abundance. They believe you are a Roman Candle of ideas.

You are the ideal choice, a model for what they feel is needed. In some ways, they want you to bring what James Collins calls, *Big, Hairy, Audacious Goals*. To be the best. To get there first. To make a difference.

Those first 120 days can be much like living with a puppy or a perfectionist— it can be messy. But you're not discouraged or dismayed. Just like the Godfather Don Vito Corleone said: "This is the job I've chosen. And there's no turning back."

You are convinced you will succeed. You see opportunities where others see threats and impossible challenges.

The future growth and vitality of the college depends on you. The spark comes from the president. You provide the electricity, the power.

You're not afraid of uncertainly or ambiguity. You embrace it. You love it. This is the epicenter of life.

John W. Gardner, in his *No Easy Victories* must have had you in mind when he wrote: "Nothing is more satisfying than to be engaged in work in which every capacity and talent you have is needed. Every lesson you may have learned is used. Every value you care about is furthered and fulfilled."

You are willing to take great risks in order to achieve great returns. You are going to be an immense success. You are going to have more fun than a van full of jugglers and clowns.

You take your cue from that revered and brilliant philosopher, Dr. Seuss:
> "And will you succeed?
> Yes! You will, indeed!
> (98 and ¾ percent guaranteed.)"

2

IT'S MAKE OR BREAK TIME
(Before Your Arrive)

There's a film by the famous French comedian, Sascha Guitry. In it, three thieves are arguing over the division of seven pearls. The pearls are worth a King's ransom.

One of the thieves hands two of the pearls to the man on his right. Then two to the man on his left.

"I will keep three," he says.

"How come you keep three?" says the man on his right.

"Because I am the leader."

"Oh, but how come you are the leader?"

"Because I have the most pearls."

That's it. You are the new president. You have the most pearls. You were chosen to lead the institution to new heights and swelling growth never before imagined. You are the leader.

Note this carefully. It is essential you get off to a proper start.

Perhaps the most valuable time you can spend is from the day you were officially appointed to the day you walk into your office for the first time as the new president.

It is a precious opportunity to learn everything you can about the college, shape expectations, and think about what will happen in the first few months you are in office. You must leverage every moment you have.

The time before you take office is of crucial consequence. Use the interval before your first official day on the campus— to prepare, learn, plan, and determine as best you can what your priorities will be.

You become a thinking machine. Designing and creating. Envisioning the changes that might seem necessary and most appropriate. If you do this ahead of time, you will create great momentum from the very start.

You get ready. You prepare for your arrival and your early days. You prepare! I think of my five Ps: Prior Preparation Prevents Poor Performance.

Be curious and daring. You will want to learn in advance as much as you possibly can. You must be ready in those first 120 days after you take office to take risks, experiment, and attempt new things. The excitement of the new position begins immediately, the day you first heard you were selected. That's also when your probing begins.

Your task during this important period before you take office is to examine, ask questions, and request information. Lots of information.

It's absolutely amazing what you don't find out when you don't ask. You can't tell how deep a puddle is until you actually step into it.

But here's the problem. You are absolutely certain you asked every conceivable question before taking the job. You thought there was nothing left to chance. Wrong!

You arrive on the campus and even on the first day you find it's not exactly what you thought it was. It doesn't matter how much you talked with someone in advance, it's just going to be different. Count on it.

That is why it is essential you do as good a job of preparation as possible. Scott D. Miller calls this period between the appointment and actually taking office, "make or break" time. He's right.

You need to have as good an understanding as possible of the college's environment and culture. This means determining its objectives, its challenges, and its strategy for meeting the days ahead. It may require several visits to the campus before you take office.

Even before your first day, you will want to challenge, test, justify, and substantiate what you hear. This will give you an opportunity in your early days to be thinking of changes that need to be made. Keep in mind, in most instances, the board expects the new president to make changes. That is why you were selected.

It's never easy. The moment you step on campus the first day, the environment and ethos of the college changes. That's not necessarily bad.

And even though you have carefully prepared for the new task, there are going to be unexpected twists and turns in the road. If you plan properly in advance, you will arrive at your destination prepared and confident. As confident, as they say, as a Methodist with 4 Aces.

The problem is that you are frantically busy phasing out of your present position. There's so much to do, a mountain-high pile of work yet to be completed. So little time.

But if you don't take the time to learn about your new assignment and the college's vision and culture, it places you at a pressing disadvantage. Before your arrival, you should understand the challenges of your new position and be thinking about the opportunities. Be thinking. Be planning.

You need to move quickly. That doesn't mean without thought and careful consideration. Here is a starting list of some of the items to review before your arrival.

1. I assume you had an attorney working with you on the negotiation of your employment agreement. It's important there is a mutual understanding of the arrangements between you and the board.

   I don't like the word *negotiate*. You and the board are on the same side— you both seek a successful future for the college. Negotiate makes it sound like it's adversarial. But keep in mind that this is the time to seek your maximum interests. The board wants you and they will reach.

2. Consider enlisting a mentor or a network of advisors you can count on. Seek those for whom you have high regard and are esteemed in the profession. It is a crime of overconfidence to feel you can take on this job on your own.

   In most cases, you can't count on anyone on the inside to be of help. Too often, you can't discuss issues that need fixing with even your senior staff. You're not always certain whose judgment you can trust in those early days.

"It ends up," says Stephen Jennings, "you really can't confide in anyone." Jennings is in his fourth presidency. He knows a thing or two.

"You talk with the chairman of the board, but even that can become difficult. The truth is you're not certain you want to let the chair know there are some things you can't handle."

Use your mentor or network during this interval be-tween your appointment and your first day in office to talk with and explore the questions you should be asking the board and some of the senior staff. If possible, use your mentor throughout your tenure.

"It's very important that you have someone to talk with," Jake Schrum tells me. "The presidency is a lonely place— even though you're surrounded by people. You need someone you can confide in, or who will just listen.

"It can be another college president you have confi-dence in or it might be a trustee. But you need someone who can listen to the issues you face and perhaps help you out. Or just be a listening post."

3. Have the board put in place a plan for the transition, from the old to the new. This can involve both trustees and staff. Let's call it the Transition Committee.

   This committee needs to be in contact with you on a regular basis so there is an understanding of their plans and yours. A representative from the college's public relations office should probably be a member of the Transition

Committee so that the announcement of your appointment and subsequent media encounters are launched like a rocket.

This isn't so much about you as it is about the college. You want the institution to receive as much positive media coverage and public relations impact as possible.

I've known of some colleges that hired a public relations firm to help with the announcements and the proper launching and design of the early days— your introduction to the college community, the special activities, the events, the major happening on the campus, and the inauguration.

4. There are plenty of important documents you will want to review in advance of your arrival. Read the Articles of Incorporation, the college's constitution, and the bylaws.

    This isn't fascinating bedtime reading, but it is important. It may require your ability to restate Athenian philosophy as if run through a Dr. Phil synthesizer.

    The Mission Statement is essential. You need not, by the way, consider this as sacred as a Papal Encyclical. One of the early things you may wish to do in your tenure is to review the Mission Statement for its currency and relevancy. May I add that if a sixth grader can understand it, you're on the right track.

    Ask for the board minutes for the past several years. This will give you a good idea of what has been happening and if there are some major issues you need to know about.

    Review all the financial documents you can get your

hands on. If you don't understand all of this, ask for help from someone who does. You are going to want the financial audits, the income and expense reports, and balance sheets for the last three fiscal years.

Thomas Dillon tells me he authorized an extensive study of the financial condition of the college before he took office. "I wanted to see what the true picture was. And it wasn't good!

"The college hadn't balanced its budget in the last five years and had not balanced it in the last eight out of ten years. There was an indebtedness no one had talked about. It's hard to believe. I had been dean of the college for ten years and didn't know anything about the financial crisis."

Read everything. Ask for the college catalogue, annual reports for the last three years, and copies of all publications they can put together and send you.

Phew! But it's all very important. If any of this material isn't available, that should be a *Red Alert* for you. That's an early warning that something is awry.

"You can't prepare too much," Scott Miller tells me. "I had them send me everything possible they could get their hands on so I could read and understand the college. I suppose I went through 75 different items."

5. Request a roster of all board members, including home addresses and phone numbers, work affiliations (title and company), with addresses, e-mail and office and mobile phone numbers.

6. Ask for an organizational chart of the senior staff. Get the names, job descriptions for these key positions, home addresses, e-mail, and phone numbers. I think you should also ask for birth dates.

7. You should visit the campus. Some I spoke with made a number of visits. It's an excellent way of getting a "feel" for your new community and campus.

    Sue DeWine and her husband made several quiet trips to the campus. They visited the community and walked around the campus. But no one knew. They came unannounced.

    "For some reason, my coming was kept a secret from the college community. I would never let that happen again. That was a big mistake. It meant that the first opportunity folks got to see me and know me was on my first day."

8. If possible, talk with the outgoing president. You don't have to accept everything as gospel. But it's important you have this discussion. Use it much as a drunk uses a lamp-post— for support rather than complete illumination.

    "In my three presidencies," Scott Miller says, "I have tried to spend at least four hours with my predecessor— and maybe a few days beyond that. I have no organized agenda. I just gently probe and ask a lot of questions."

    I know of some boards that plan for a transition of several months. I think this is totally unnecessary, usually unwanted by the new president, and can actually be an impediment.

9. Get as much statistical information as you possibly can on the key issues. Take, for instance, student enrollment (FTE), retention, number of inquiries converted into actual admissions. Percentage of alumni giving. Attrition and retention of gifts. The endowment.

   You get the idea. You will want to see all of this for the past five years.

10. Ask for a calendar of all important future events you need to get into your schedule for the coming year.

11. Subscribe to the newspaper of the community you're moving to.

12. Check all possible Web sites that will help you understand your new environment. You most likely reviewed your college's Web before you were selected. Choose three or four comparable colleges to see how yours rates.

13. If there isn't a President's Home or you are not planning on using it, ask some board members for the name of a real estate agent they can recommend.

14. If there is an interim president, you should call every two or three weeks. It's a great way to check-in and find out what's happening

   I also suggest calling your board chair on some sort of a regular basis with any questions you might have. Or just call to let the chair know of the progress you are making in your orientation. But, of course, don't be a pest.

15. Find out if there has been a comprehensive study or an institutional audit of some sort that is current.

I refer to an outside team that provided an objective and candid assessment of the college in all of its vital components.

Here is why this is important. You want an outside group to peel back all of the layers and get to the very nub of any issues that might exist. This calls for a professional team headed by a senior consultant.

If this hasn't been done before your arrival, you may ask (insist if you feel bold!) that it be completed before you take office. The timing is important. You have nothing at all at stake of the past, and you have nothing to prove.

16. If the college has been through an Accreditation in the past three years, ask to see the documentation the institution prepared and the Accreditation Team's Report.

Georgia Nugent read everything she could get her hands on about the college in the first five months before she actually took office. This included a comprehensive history. William Faulkner said, "The past is never dead. It is never even the past."

Georgia tells me the last Accreditation Study Report was her most significant reading. This represented some of the most revealing and important information.

17. Don't be afraid to say you don't know the answer. Or you don't understand. Or you want more information. You have a right to all the information. Everything you need should be made immediately available.

Investigate everything. Just as a *sous* chef peels an onion layer by layer. Open every closed door.

18. After you have digested all of this, it's a good time to begin thinking of the major challenges the college faces— at least as you envision them at this time. That's an appropriate discussion to have when you talk with the board chair.

> Review with the chair some of the opportunities that now exist and will likely exist in the future. (I had a friend at GE who told me, "At GE, we were never allowed to use the word *problem*. We always had to talk about opportunities. But at times, we had a helluva lot of opportunities."

> Ask if there are any issues of great urgency you may have to face when you arrive. Find out how the college is addressing these challenges. Is there anything in place now it is doing to work through the issues, or is this something you have to take on immediately on your arrival.

It's perfectly acceptable to talk with the appropriate people (board chair, senior officers, your mentor, others) to determine what needs to happen to take advantage of the most promising, unexploited opportunities for the future.

What's interesting is that most of the presidents I spoke with took on their engagement in a college that was either in a crisis or in a period of significant transition. They tell me about the dangers of making high stake changes without very extensive advance preparation.

If you aren't ready when you arrive, it can be like flying an airplane blind in a storm and none of your instruments is working. It may turn out okay. You may make it. But you've never been in a storm like this before and the potential to crash is great. You can't go on instinct or even experience. You must prepare.

This is the excitement and the fun of it. You are involved in deep discovery, a fascinating adventure. It's exhilarating— even if the news is at times discouraging or even devastating. You will be a success.

Keep in mind Maya Angelou's comment: "You did what you knew how to do, and when you knew better you did better." And now after all this review, you know better.

Here are 14 things to remember as you prepare for your arrival and the first 120 days:

1   The value of your time.
2   The success of perseverance.
3   The joy of working hard.
4   The example you set for quality.
5   The inspiration of a smile.
6   The worth of character and integrity.
7   The power of kindness.
8   The obligation of duty to the college.
9   The influence of your presidential example.
10 The necessity of having time to think.
11 The virtue of patience when necessary.
12 The importance of listening.
13 The obligation to relax – the job should be fun.
14 And remember, CEO does not stand for Career Education is Over.

You are now ready for the first 120 days in office. You will have a triumphant tenure. To use Hemingway's prophecy, you are, "the winner and still the undisputed champion."

Oh, and one last thing to remember: You were appointed, not anointed.

3

IT BEGINS
(Your First Days)

You have arrived.

You have found the way to your new office. This is the start of the 120 days. It is the first day of life in your new position. You have nothing to remember. Everything to hope for.

Where do you begin? It is well to keep in mind the instructions on the back of the Hellman's Mayonnaise jar: Keep cool and don't freeze.

As you begin this wondrous journey in your new surroundings, I'll start you off with some points to remember. They're from James L. Fisher.

But first let me tell you something about Jim Fisher. He is very likely higher education's most outstanding spokesperson. He is author of a dozen or so books on presidential leadership, board involvement and responsibility, and academic quality. He backs it all up with empirical data combined with his own opinion (he's never in doubt).

I've known Jim for years and years, when we were both young. He was young and wise. Over all that time, I never grew younger. But he seemed to always grow wiser.

Here is Jim's list of things to remember as you begin your first days. I've added a few points to Jim's.

1. Remember, in everything you do, in every decision you make— it's all about the students.

2. Relax. After you're gone a year or two, you will not be missed. Few will even remember you.

3. You are the president. You are the leader, whether the office fits comfortably at first or not.

4. Never get off the presidential platform. Always keep a presidential presence.

5. Never act beneath your office or hide behind your office.

6. To acquire knowledge you must study— but to acquire wisdom, you must observe.

7. You may find yourself racing in circles. Keep in mind the world is round and the place that seems like the end may only be the beginning.

8. Stand when you speak. If you do it right, only you will know your feet are in moving sand.

9. At least once a week, show up where you are least expected.

10. Be plenty serious about the position, but never about yourself.

11. Be like the comely swan. Above the surface, composed and calm, a thing of beauty to behold. But below the surface, paddling like hell.

12. There's going to be pressure. You can count on that. There may be times when it may be difficult to keep your emotional balance. You may feel you are drowning with all that is going on, and somehow aren't able to break the surface for air.

Even though you have accomplished great deal the first 120 days, it really is a marathon, not a 100-yard dash. Keep everything in its proper place.

Take care of the present, but keep your mind and eyes focused on the long term objectives.

13. Enjoy the presidency. If it's not fun, it's not worth it. Have fun. I preach Thoreau's doctrine: do what you love.

14. Back to that first Dictum— it's all about students.

You're not going to be able to accomplish everything you hoped. You mustn't give the feeling to others of being a whirling dervish. Not everything is urgent or an emergency. One sure way to get high blood pressure is to go mountain climbing over molehills.

Keep a single minded focus on those few vital priorities that simply must be achieved. Not everything is essential. You need to have some understanding about when and how your priorities are to be implemented. And by whom.

The course of a railway train is uniquely prescribed for it at most points of its journey by the rails on which it runs. Here and there, however, it comes to a junction. At that intersection, alternate courses are open to it. The train may be turned on to one or another course by an expenditure of energy involved in moving the rails. Your job is to move the rails.

Start by taking a careful look of the organizational architecture of your college. In those first few months, you need to make decisions about your senior people, and whether the organization structure is in place the way you want it.

Here's what is of great consequence. You must decide whether the team you inherited is the right one and is appropriate to get the job done. Be wary of anyone on the senior staff who doesn't share your excitement and commitment. As Chesterton once observed, "Enthusiasts soon understand one another."

If you feel changes must be made, determine how to put that process in motion. Don't delay. This will be among the most important decisions you make. It's the static that can crack and crackle in your tenure.

"In the first days, you meet with your senior administrators. You make certain they understand what you're all about. You gain their respect." That's Bruce Heilman talking.

"You begin right away taking their measure. You determine who is competent. If they are not, you may have to make early decisions about their tenure. You need to make certain they are willing to work hard and share your vision."

You want a senior staff that is realistic— but confident, optimistic, and audacious. I've seen it happen at senior staff meetings. There is one word that blocks action, poisons motivation, and smothers any chance for success and growth. That killer word is: *can't*.

In those early days, it is well to define your immediate objectives and some of the goals you seek down the road a bit— perhaps three to six months in the future. Be thinking about how you will begin to seek some early wins. That's important. You want to create action that builds your credibility and establishes a sense of momentum.

Identify the key initiatives and resources necessary to pursue those objectives. This may mean designing a plan for the restructuring of your senior team. You must do what you must do.

When you take on your role of the new president, it means leaving behind the confines of what you know how to do well. That's true even if it was another college presidency.

The sea changes. It can be like navigating an obsolete vessel past unchartered reefs in unfamiliar waters.

The environment is different. Those protectors of the hoary culture of the college are keeping a sleepless vigil. The campus is awash with rumors, murmurs, and speculation.

You are embarking on what can often become an uncomfortable journey. The territory can be unknown, uncertain, and perilous. You are one with Indiana Jones who claimed, "We are faced with insurmountable opportunity. I'm just not certain what my next move should be."

You are moving from a position where you understood the environment and culture (or at least thought you did!). Now, all of the connective tissues have to be understood. Some need to be rebuilt.

Perhaps one of your most important priorities is to change the culture. Your college may have been suffering from a stillness of time.

What the board may have been hoping in selecting you was to have you act like an unstable air mass, a sudden storm that blows all the windows open. This may very well be the reason you were hired even though it was never stated.

"There is indeed a very special culture at Kenyon," Georgia Nugent says. "There is a strong sense of *The Kenyon Way*. What I heard often was: 'This is not Kenyon. This is not the Kenyon Way.' That is most often the statement I heard in the early days when someone didn't like something I was proposing."

There is no single formula. That's the worst of it. No prescribed and proven routes you can take. Only some suggestions. None of the situations are the same. There is no formula to most effectively manage the move into your new position.

There are only ideas that have worked for others in many situations. But each college is different and that's the knot. Your approach will inevitably be shaped by the situations you now face and have faced, your prior experience, the board's anticipation, and your particular leadership style.

"I didn't really want to change the culture or the college," Sue DeWine tells me. "I simply wanted to enhance it."

The changing of the guard and the challenges it poses can be intimidating for the new president. "In the middle of the journey of this life, I was traveling through a dark woods," begins the *Divine Comedy*. The transition of the old to a new president is obviously a critical time for the college, also.

Trifling differences in your actions (or lack of activity) can have an extraordinary impact on how you are viewed. At times, these are totally disproportionate to their actual importance. That is why the first 120 days are so critical.

If there is a lack of momentum, your college community perceives it. A failure to demonstrate dynamic leadership, or moments of indecision, can create a challenging, uphill battle for the rest of your tenure.

You spend a great deal of time before taking office, as I recommended earlier, learning as much as you possibly can about the college. Sadly, you will find there is so much more they didn't tell you and that you don't know.

You are going to discover that you are surrounded by people day and night, and everyone wants a piece of you. But there are few you can really confide in.

You feel like you are running up the down escalator. Welcome to the club.

You are confronted with committee meetings, faculty sessions, discussions with senior staff, and calls with board members. You walk the campus and talk with every student you contact.

As busy as you are, you are going to find it a lonely job. I'm reminded of a Buddhist legend of a young farmer going upstream in a rowboat to deliver his produce to the village. He was in a hurry. It was a hot day and he wanted to make his delivery and get home before dark.

As he looked ahead, he spied a large vessel, heading rapidly downstream toward his rowboat. The large boat was heading straight at him. He rowed furiously to get out of the way, but it didn't seem to help.

He yelled at the other boat, "Change direction, you idiot! You're going to hit me. The river is plenty wide. Be careful."

His screaming was to no avail. The other vessel hit his boat with a sickening thud. His rowboat was sliced in two. The farmer was enraged and yelled, "You moron! How can you manage to hit my boat in the middle of this wide river? What is wrong with you?"

As he looked at the other vessel, he realized that there was no one in the other boat. He was screaming at an empty vessel that had broken free of its moorings and was going downstream with the current.

The lesson is simple. For the President, there is often no one in the other boat. You are all by yourself. It can be lonely. It can be very lonely. At times, you are looking with hope at an empty vessel.

With all of the face to face and talking that you do, you actually have no one to talk with. Not anyone with whom you can share your deepest concerns and thoughts. That's why I suggested earlier having a mentor.

For some presidents, the new position places them in a crisis of expectations. If that is your situation, you require an electrifying versatility. The job assails you, penetrates you, molds you.

There must be the brutal and immediate assimilation of learning and understanding. This requires that you are a person of action and decisiveness, as well as reflection and compassion. That's an extraordinary combination— sort of a mix of a Jack Welch and a Mother Theresa.

You may find yourself in what Erich Fromm (the New School) called, "the struggle against pointlessness." You can identify with that. With all your meetings and discussions, you find yourself caught in the awful maze created by aimlessness and its cousins, inaction and postponement.

You're poised for important and exciting action. But everyone else wants to discuss the matter. At length. God so loved the world, he did not send a committee.

I am told that you don't motivate people by telling them hell is a place in which they will burn. You motivate them by telling them that hell is an unending committee meeting.

I find in the colleges I work with, the best presidents are a bit restless by nature, never satisfied, and aware there is no such thing as perfection. But they always seek excellence in everything they and the college do.

The successful presidents see great opportunities, brilliantly disguised as impossible predicaments. They yield to the Chinese maxim: "The situation is totally hopeless— but not serious."

The successful presidents understand their college is not static. Remember Walt Whitman's injunction: "Make it happen now." There is always something happening (sometimes frightening things). They are convinced any situation can be improved and any procedure upgraded.

You need to envision in fairly concrete terms what you want to do and where you want to go in those first days. You will wish input from every important source. But in the end, it is your vision that will determine the journey.

"I had done sufficient study in preparing for my first days. I actually had a vision for what I wanted to achieve." I'm with John Hood. He continues. "Before I even arrived, I began working on a planning document. I finished it in the first week I was on campus. That evolved into a five-year plan."

Think about planning a trip. You figure out where you want to go. Then you decide your form of transportation. Finally, you determine how to get there. If this is all new, you may have to make it up as you go along.

That's all right. You need not know all the details. You maintain a certain amount of flexibility and begin thinking about who are the people you want to go on the ride with you. It requires a historical perspective and an appreciation of the institution's character and values.

This is your journey. Your trip. You have a striking commitment to work arduous hours to achieve mighty objectives.

The early failures of a president are rarely fatal. But to not make the attempt is the great failure. A person never fails who never tries. Objectives that aren't met are not the great failures in life. The great tragedy is not having objectives.

At times it may seem like diving from the high board. It's true that experience is the best teacher. But sometimes the tuition is awfully high.

When you're thinking, "I'm going to give up"— Hope whispers, "Try it one more time."

Presidential genius is the infinite capacity for taking pains. The job offers no guarantees— only opportunities, unpredictability, and challenges disguised as problems. Where there is no pain, there is no momentum. Remember, steel is tempered by the fire.

Over the first 120 days, it will seem like you were consistently caught up in the *thick of thin things*. You are a one-person fire department, putting out fires and rescuing the college from dire circumstances. It is, as they say, like drinking from a fire hose.

The effective president chooses to succeed. You don't stumble upon success. You choose it. There is a healthy impatience and discontent with anything less than a zenith performance.

"Work hard, take chances, be very bold," says a character in the movie *Julia*. Indecision will be your enemy. Consider a lack of energy and momentum as traitors to your success.

You serve as a model. You symbolize the college's vision and future. You carry the message. Your impact is without bounds. You write psalms of passion and celebration.

You won't always be successful in those first 120 days. You won't be as mature and knowledgeable in your thinking as you will be later on. There may be days you trip and tumble, blunder and bungle. It happens. There will be days like that.

Don't be afraid to say you made a mistake. A board member, a veteran Navy pilot, told me once: Never run out of altitude, air speed, ideas, or options.

How the devil do you accomplish all that must be done. The pressure is intense, particularly in those first 120 days. Nothing is difficult if you divide it into small jobs. How do you eat an elephant? A bite at a time.

You are the president. The music maker. You are the dreamer of dreams. The risk taker. The decision maker. Don't worry about stumbling. Remember the old Frank Sinatra refrain: "Each time you find yourself flat on your face, pick yourself up and get back in the race."

You remain inquisitive, curious about everything. For you, in these first 120 days, everything is about making the proper institutional connections. Read everything, you observe, walk the campus, talk to students, and visit with faculty. Explore. Probe. Ask questions.

There aren't enough hours in the day. But somehow you manage. You are forced to remember Jesse Ventura's memorable line from the movie *Predator*: "I don't have time to bleed!"

I give some suggestions in the chapters that follow on specific topics you need to handle in your first 120 days. But for now, let me propose:

1. Follow the dictum of Tiger Woods: "I start every day thinking that I have a great chance to win."

2. Decide exactly what you want to achieve. It is the indispensable first step. Determine what you hope to accomplish in the first 120 days, in the first year, in the next two years.

3. Write down your objectives. Be specific. If you do not have a precise target, you will hit it with remarkable success.

4. If you can conceive it, you can achieve it. If you can dream it, Walt Disney said, you can do it.

5. Be willing to pay the price.

6. Design a comprehensive plan.

7. Determine how to take action on your plan.

8. Prepare. Prepare. Prepare. Change. Growth and success favor the mind that is best prepared.

9. Develop a written detailed calendar.

10. Do something every day to meet your objectives.

11. Follow the plan. Make the calendar time-imperative.

12. Never give up. Don't let anyone dampen your dreams.

13. And finally, place a prominent sign in your office where you see it everyday: **"IT'S ALL ABOUT THE STUDENTS."**

4

GET READY,
GET SET...
(You Begin The Journey)

If it was in your power, how would you build a frog? Would you try to emulate the unusual croak? Or the extraordinary leap? Or the prodigious eyes?

No.

In all likelihood, you would study the pond.

These are your first days on the campus, in your new office. How will you study the pond?

You need to climb the learning curve as fast as you possibly can. Everyone is watching to see what you will do. They critique your actions and take apart your words. Then, there are all those decisions that have to be made.

This means understanding the college's mission, services, culture, and structure. At times, it will seem like you're navigating the ocean in a rowboat. Hopefully, you had a good start on examining the college in detail before your arrival.

Transitions are times of perilous vulnerability. But also occasion for unlimited and monumental opportunity. It's what E.B. White called, "the vibrations of great times and tall deeds."

John Hood had four months between his election and his first day in office. That gave him a good bit of time to prepare. He decided to visit some universities he thought were comparable to Oxford University in terms of issues and the character of the university.

He went to the University of Glasgow, University of Reading, University of Toronto, University of Vancouver, Stanford University, and University of Melbourne. He spent three or four days at each.

"Those visits to other universities were extremely helpful," John says. "This is something I would recommend to anybody starting a new post."

(Go back. Reread John's last comment. I don't want you to take that casually. It is a suggestion of profound and echoing significance to you. This could very well be one of the most important learning experiences, easily available to you, as you prepare to take office.)

Choose three or four colleges you feel are comparable to yours in character and size. Spend two or three days at each, visiting the president and some of her senior staff.)

When he was in his new position at Oxford, Hood walked around the campus every day. In the first few months, he visited each of the university's 39 colleges. He sat in on lectures, attended cocktail parties, and spoke at every opportunity possible. There were probably 50 speeches in the first 120 days.

Mary Pat Seurkamp worked day and night in the early days. She walked the campus and ate in the dining hall every day she was at the college. That was so important an experience, she continues to do so.

"Those first 120 days were terribly important. I spent most of the time meeting with people, asking questions, and listening. I made contact with as many as I could— students, faculty, and staff.

"One of the things a president has to learn to do is to listen a great deal. Probe and listen. I think the reason some presidents fail is that they get caught up in small matters and are too removed from what is really going on, too far removed from the students, and they don't spend enough time listening."

At times, it can feel like you're trying to bag a live platypus. Listen to what Stephen Jennings says.

"It can be exhausting. In those early days, I was on the go all the time, going in a hundred different directions. You need to be totally engaged every moment.

"You are being torn apart. You somehow have to find time for yourself. But there is no time. You go to all events, all the activities. On top of all that's going on with campus events, you get involved with a lot of local things in the community."

Scott Miller says it takes immense energy. "In the early months, I not only walked the campus every day, but I met with people individually, in small group meetings, and in clusters. I attended a number of alumni meetings. I wanted folks to know my vision for the college.

"I met with every board member at their home or office. That was extremely helpful. I got to know their frame of mind and I wanted them to understand my agenda.

"In the first few weeks, I received 830 e-mails that came from a variety of people. I answered every single one of them by either another e-mail or a personal call when that seemed appropriate.

"A personal call went to those I felt were the most valuable. I let them know how pleased I was with their e-mail. When I called, you can imagine how excited they were to hear from me.

"In those first 120 days," Joseph White tells me, "time is of the essence. I went to see every trustee, every person who reported to me, every major donor, and all of the key friends of the university. At the University of Illinois, that's a lot of visits. But it's absolutely essential.

"I went to see key faculty. I would go to them instead of having them come to my office. I think that's good strategy for a lot of reasons. For one thing, I get to see their surroundings and how they keep their office. But it also allows me to leave when I feel ready to do so. You learn a lot by visiting them."

In the first few weeks, Richard Jewell spent a great deal of time walking the campus. He still does. He's very visible. He watches students practice their sports, he goes to all activities and all events.

In his very first week, on a Wednesday, he went to the Student Union in the afternoon. He sat at a table with his coffee. Students started coming over to him to talk. He still does this every Wednesday. They come by the dozens.

Ed Koch, the former Mayor of New York, gave this advice to the new incoming Mayor: "Do all the parades." As a new President you need to be visible and present at everything. E.M. Forster was writing to you: "Spend all your time connecting. Simply connect."

During Sue DeWine's first few weeks, she met with over 400 people to talk about her dreams for the college. She laid out her objectives. She spent a great deal of time listening to students during those early weeks.

"I was with students an enormous amount of time. They weren't happy with what had been happening at the college. I became their sounding board.

"I listened to their peeves, their problems, and their issues with the college. But I also heard about their hopes for the future and what they felt they needed to get from the college. Those early days became a wonderful experience for me and I believe all the students."

Sue still spends a great deal of time with students. She invites them to the president's home for all sorts of occasions. Last Halloween, for instance, they came in costumes. They came by the hundreds.

She goes to everything. Every possible activity and event. It started on her very first day on campus. I spoke to one of her students. He told me, "The president is everywhere." As far as Sue is concerned, it's all about the students.

Now, I'm going to tell you something that may be a bit sensitive. I only tell this story because it underlines the importance of visiting and being visible. I won't mention the name. He is now at another college.

One of the presidents I spoke with told me this story. Her predecessor had been on the campus for 30 years, and president for 20 of those. During his last few years . . . well, it was a pretty quiet time for him. That's the truth of it. He hadn't been seen at many college events.

When the new president attended an art show in her early months, the art faculty was absolutely delighted. They pointed out that her predecessor had not been to one of these shows in years, not one that they could ever remember.

The new president made points with the art faculty, but that wasn't the objective. She loves her job and she loves students. For her, being a college president is an invitation to life's dance.

Don't be surprised if at times you feel your life is being lived like a play. You sense you are an actor on stage being driven by directions and actions not your own. James Johnson can attest to that.

"As I look back now, I wish I had slowed down a bit. But I don't know how I would have accomplished all I did if I had. I was visiting people all the time, speaking to groups, meeting trustees, and talking with donors.

"I recognized I wasn't at my best and wasn't spending any time at home. But I didn't know how to stop. The train was moving too fast and I couldn't jump off.

"There was simply too much to do. I recognize now I was concentrating on problems instead of opportunities. I've changed that now. But if you're putting out fires, that's what you have to do. The trouble was that every time I put out a fire, a new blaze would start somewhere else."

You are going to be humming that tune from the wonderful play, *On The Town*:

> "Where has all the time gone to?
> Haven't done half the things I want to.
> Oh well, I'll catch up
> Some other time."

It was the same for all. Georgia Nugent sums it up. "In the first 120 days, I was so busy, so new to it all, everything seems like a blur now." As the old country song goes, "I didn't know whether to kill myself or go bowling."

There are hundreds of successful transitions each year by new presidents. There are, also, a small handful of examples of very talented leaders, some with sterling records of performance, who stumble along the way. They become mired in what Thoreau referred to as, "the mud and slush of the opinion, tradition, and delusion of the do-nothing people."

Yours will be one of the triumphant transitions. That is a promise.

All at once, you're ready to begin. You roll up your sleeves. You take a deep breath. And here goes.

You stand at the beginning of the greatest day. The day is not a gift, but a prize. You will not capture the prize until you have won it.

Heed the wisdom of Ralph Waldo Emerson. He said: "Finish every day and be done with it. You have done what you could. Some blunders and absurdities no doubt crept in. Forget them as soon as you can.

"Tomorrow is a new day. Begin it well and calmly, and with too high a spirit to be encumbered with your old nonsense.

"This new day is all that is good and fair. It is too dear, with its hopes and invitations, to waste a moment on yesterdays."

In those early days, if your actions are correct, no one remembers. If they're wrong, no one forgets. There will be times when you think seriously about the choice of the protagonist in Beckett's *The Unnamable*— will it be the dagger or the poison.

You bring passion and energy to those early days. It pains you when you see mediocrity. You exalt when you find high quality and exciting expectations from others. You have an appetite for the future.

In the first few months, you remind me a bit, in those early days of an Evangelist. Like them, you are transforming lives. You convey profound and passionate beliefs.

You help people see the best in themselves. Like the Evangelist, you touch lives in wondrous ways. You are always challenging yourself, going through agonizing self-evaluation, raising your own personal bar.

No one is a harsher critic of you than yourself. You seem to thrive on no sleep, you are a compulsive reader, you retain everything, and you consume so much caffeine you make coffee nervous.

I find often that the great dividing line between success and failure can be stated in six words: "I did not take the time."

Keep in mind what Steve Covey says in his *The Seven Habits of Highly Effective People*. What each of us needs, he tells us, every day is a personal victory. The earlier in the day you get it, the more the rest of the day will be like delicious icing on a cake.

A word of warning. Your office is a dangerous place to spend the first 120 days.

You have perhaps heard about the college president who came out of his office on February 2nd. He saw his own shadow and ran back to the office. He was never seen again.

A common refrain I heard from all I spoke with was the need to get out and meet as many people as soon as possible. Everyone stressed that. This means all sorts of people. Trustees, donors, faculty, staff, students, the grounds staff, leaders in the community, the works.

You are torn. You need to be out meeting all of these people. At the same time, you have to be on campus as much as possible and accessible to everyone. That doesn't mean by the way, making yourself completely available.

I worry about those who take pride in their "open door" policy. That means they make themselves completely available. There are too many opportunities for indiscriminate contact with anyone who simply wants to be at your doorstep.

What you want is to be approachable, but not completely accessible. There's a great distinction.

Most of the presidents I spoke with don't spend much time behind the desk. When I wrote earlier that you want to meet everyone, let me tell you about Jake Schrum.

"One of the things I did on one of the first days I was in office was to go to the donut shop in town. I bought donuts and coffee for the grounds and maintenance staff. I sat down with them and just started talking. I spent an hour and half with them.

"The campus was in terrible shape. I wanted them to know how important I felt they were to the institution. I met with them regularly in those early days. It was the talk of the campus that I would take time to do that. By the way, the grounds improved dramatically almost immediately.

"Even now," Jake goes on, "I go into the dining hall every lunchtime I have available. I just spot a table where there's an open seat and I go over to the table and I say, 'Do you mind if I sit with you?'" The students are absolutely delighted.

"If I find that I have an open spot in my calendar during the day, even for 15 or 20 minutes, I take off for a walk." Jake says he walks the campus regularly.

"It's wonderful being able to greet students and call them by name. They like seeing me around. I walk in the evening with my wife. Especially in the early days. That becomes very special for students to see us on the campus in the evening. We stop and chat with everyone we can."

In his very first day, Evans Whitaker went to the cafeteria to sit with students. He continues to do that every day he is on the campus. Students know they can come and sit with him and visit.

It is the great compromise. You want to spend as much time with students as you possibly can. That's what it is all about. That's why you became president. The students. It's what Faubert referred to as, "The main dish of existence."

But you know in those first few weeks, first few months, you must be out making contacts.

Lisa Marsh Ryerson tells me that she was away from the office virtually full time.

"Within the first 120 days, whatever tone you set is what you end up keeping. Immediately, when I took office, the second or third day, I went to see the college attorney and the college auditor. I wanted to know as much as I possibly could about our situation.

"When you're president, there is no privacy. But I didn't want to spend very much time in my office. This is especially true in the first 120 days. Your life is totally consumed by work and much of it away from the college. And when you are on campus, you're greeting students, attending activities, and being visible in a hundred different places.

"I walked the campus. I wanted to be seen as much as I possibly could. I was everywhere. Lincoln spent a lot of time during the war walking around with his troops. I believe that's a good example."

There are times when you don't even have time to walk around the campus. James Johnson says that in the first few weeks, he nearly wiped himself out doing the necessary fundraising. He was going everywhere, all the time, in all directions. Bigger than life— like Gulliver among the Lilliputians.

"I never worked harder. I knew that if we did not raise $2 million immediately, we would have to close. I called on major friends. I made 12 calls in the very first week. I lived in a storm."

Johnson spent several weeks meeting with board members and major corporations. He didn't totally neglect his need to be on the campus. But he was torn. He needed to be away raising money. And he needed to be with his students.

"I met with students. I met hundreds. I attended every athletic event. I walked the halls. I walked the campus. I went to special events. Softball games. I ate in the cafeteria. I met with student officers.

"The students are important, but you also have to know your faculty. I went to see all of the faculty. I met all of them. In groups and individually. Mostly, I went to see them in their offices or I met them in the cafeteria.

"When I went to the college, I found a dispirited and discouraged faculty. They had lost faith in the college. I believed my major job was to give them hope. I met with every department. I had to let them know we were going to make it. I was a roaring optimist. Even at times when I didn't feel quite that positive inside."

Not every situation is as desperate as Johnson's, living one minute 'til midnight.

But many are. There are times for every new president, no matter how good the situation, when it's what John Steinbeck described as, "the urge to be someplace else."

The lesson, and I heard this from every president I visited with, is that you have got to get away from the office. Not necessarily the campus— I mean your office and your desk.

The failed president spends all of his time in the office. The desk is indeed a perilous place if you wish to be the visible and approachable president you know you should be.

You cannot learn to skate without first looking ridiculous. Becoming a new college president, like skating, can be slippery. You will fall down and get up numerous times. Those first 120 days can be slippery and unstable. They can also be totally exhausting.

I was on the campus of a small college in North Carolina. I was with the president. I thought he looked unusually tired.

"No sleep?" I asked.

"No, that's not it. My dilemma," the president said, "is that I've never learned to say *no!*"

Well that can be a vexing problem. Either wanting to please everyone or not being able to make a decision. This is the Tweedledum and the Tweedledee of a flawed and failing president.

Life is extremely complicated. This is particularly true on a college campus for the new president. There's never enough time and the president has to travel down too many roads, too fast, and often with no road signs.

There are the committee meetings, solving problems, fundraising, dealing with an irate donor, handling a ticklish parent-student situation, and the hundreds of other interruptions.

You end up spending 90 percent of your time taking care of those ulcer-producing intrusions. And the other 90 percent trying to do those things you feel are most important.

But the difficulty isn't the ability to say *no*. The answer is to be selective. The presidents who have a successful affect on the college community are those who learn to say *yes*— but only to those questions and decisions that count.

I think of the beautifully spinning top. It loses its momentum little by little. The circles become wider and wider, and then wobbly. The top waggles and waddles. Then finally slows to a stop and lies on its side. That reminds me of some of the presidents who are out of control.

They don't choose and select. They find after a short time their work becomes wider and wobbly. They slow to a stop. Then, lie on their side.

No one said that being a new college president is an easy job. When I asked Joseph White how he finds the time to do the myriad of activities he is called on to handle— both the outside functions as well as managing one of the largest university systems in the nation, he said: "I don't find the time. I *make* the time."

For the new president, there are going to be times of stress and pressure. Follow the wise advice Stuart Little gave the repair lineman who he meets in a ditch alongside the road (*Charlotte's Web*). "I wish you fair skies, enjoy your work, and keep a tight grip."

5

IT'S DECISION TIME
(Trust Your Impulses)

James Fisher says there are two characteristics that are of the greatest importance during the first 120 days: visibility and delivery. By delivery, he means making decisions, and making them promptly.

"If the new president is the kind who says, 'I'm going to wait to get the lay of the land.'— that's going to be a serious problem. The new president needs to start working on the very first day and begin making the necessary decisions."

You are going to be faced with decisions. Here's something I think you will find helpful.

The toughest of decisions and the right answers are almost always the ones you come to when you just sit down and say: Okay, what are we trying to do? What are the right values to guide that decision? What is going to be ultimately right for the students— because that's what it's all about.

You ignore all the politics. You ignore the screaming and the shouting.

The screaming and shouting. That's what gnaws. You have the screamers and the shouters on your campus. Every campus does. They catch you walking across the quadrangle, or they bust into your office, or they find you in a quiet moment in the cafeteria.

They have an agenda which is very seldom yours. But there's no stopping them.

> Never in question,
> Never in doubt—
> They run in circles,
> And scream and shout.

You determine what the problems are. That's where it begins. Then you need to decide whether you're turning your back on them, solving them, or making them worse. Be certain you test your basic assumptions.

You won't get kudos if your response to someone with a difficult issue is: "I don't have a solution, but I admire your problem." You have to watch out for phony solutions anyway. If you hear a quack, duck.

Jim Fisher tells me about one president he worked with who started off poorly in the first 120 days. It got worse after that. "He made brilliant decisions, but they were all the wrong decisions."

"When I was interviewed by the board," Sue DeWine says, "I told them I was a change agent. That's what they said they wanted. And when I arrived, I found that's what they really needed.

"They were hurting terribly. Finances were in shambles. That was caused mostly by poor enrollment. I had to solve the financial issue and at the same time deal with a serious declining enrollment problem.

"I had to make a lot of decisions fast. My first job was to make major cuts. The college had been using their endowment to balance the budget.

"I think one of your earliest decisions is whether you can trust the chief financial officer. It turns out in this case, I could. He knew what had to be done. He just needed some guidance."

In those first 120 days, you are going to have to make a number of decisions. Out of necessity and for a variety of reasons, many of these will be often short of any assured certainty.

I'm not sure you can be inch-perfect on any decision. The problem is if it is correct, no one remembers. If it's wrong, no one forgets.

Often, there simply isn't the time or the resources to get all the information you wish you had. Most of the time, it's not really possible.

Keep in mind that in making decisions, the true failure is not making a decision at all. All of the actions of a successful president are bold and courageous. The attempt is glorious. Even failure.

If that happens, don't be afraid to say 'I made a mistake.' If you admit to a mistake, people are quick to forgive.

Gather as much information as you possibly can. If you end up with perhaps 80 percent of what you need, you're fortunate. Most often in those early days, you won't even have that much.

Review all the information and then take your best shot and go for it.

Failure is an orphan. This may happen. Actually in most cases, it doesn't matter whether the decision is to *go* or *not go*. Either one can work. It's a delay in the decision that is fatal.

The important thing is that you mustn't postpone. There's no perfect time to make the decision. Do it now. Make that your credo.

Nothing will ever be attempted if all possible objections must first be overcome. Follow my dictum: TNT (Today Not Tomorrow).

It doesn't seem fair, but in the first few months there can be a disproportionate impact on the overall success or failure of your tenure in the years that follow. Those first 120 days are a pivotal period. You will feel like a tired swimmer in the waves of time.

Esther Barrazone tells me in the first 120 days you are committed to making major decisions. Some have to be made on the spot. Immediately.

"You have to work quickly and decisively. Learning, learning, learning as much as you can about the situation. But at times, there isn't even a minute to think it through. You have to make a decision. Getting as good a handle on things as you can is what you work at.

"In the first few weeks, I decided I had to make a change in my senior staff. I had a director of development I had worked with before at another college. I brought her to Chatham. She is wonderful.

"I had another senior staff person I really should have fired. I waited too long. That person became an obstacle to all new development at the college. Finally, he had to go. That was a decision I should have made in those early days.

"Let me tell you about one really tough decision I had to make. And no one could do it for me. I decided we had to return a major gift to a foundation, one of the largest the college had received up to that time. As you can imagine, this was not an easy decision.

"The college had not spent the funds the way it promised and the way the Foundation wanted it done. I went to them and told them the truth. I asked if they wanted to have their money back.

"They were great. They said I could keep the funds. I told them if I could keep the grant, I would like to put it into an improved admissions process or into a new international program. They were delighted and decided on the latter. As you can imagine, that grew into a wonderful working relationship with the Foundation. They knew we could be trusted.

"There was another decision I had to make very quickly. But it was an easy one. There had been some talk about a merger with another college. That's because ours was in such terrible shape. The board didn't want a merger and neither did I. We decided emphatically against it."

Those early days are a wonderful time to make significant decisions. Rigid organizational patterns can be easily reshaped, decreased, or changed entirely. The college community is actually expecting some change. Perhaps with some trepidation. But they know it's coming.

John Hood says that even though he did a great deal of preparation in advance of his first day at Oxford, when he went there he realized there had to be significant organizational changes. He was ready.

"I made the decisions about the organization of the staff immediately. The one thing I knew was that the academic environment and quality was totally in place and nothing had to be changed there.

"I didn't realize until I actually arrived at Oxford that the university had a lot of serious issues. There were some great difficulties. Some changes that had to be made.

"When you go into a new situation, you don't know who to trust. You try to be as selective as you possibly can in choosing those you want to get information from. You gather as much data as you can. Then you make the decision. And you have to live with it.

"The one person I counted on most of all was a brilliant academician who really didn't have a great deal at stake at the university except his love for Oxford. He was one of our most senior academicians. He was very helpful.

"I had to make some major decisions about letting people go. These were obvious. These were done very early. I feel I'm compassionate, but firm.

"One of the areas I reviewed very early, perhaps in the first month, was the budget of the university. There hadn't been figures presented for six or seven months. That was a Red Light to me. I considered that a major issue. That's when I decided that the chief financial officer had to go.

"I reviewed all of the capital needs. I realized early that we had to have a major capital campaign. I began the planning for that immediately.

"Every day was hard yards. There wasn't a day that went by where there weren't difficult decisions that had to be made. Fortunately, I was willing to make them. I didn't fret, I didn't stew. I made the decisions and then went on."

For some, that's easier said than done. It's a vulnerable time. You don't have as much knowledge about the college as you would like, and as much as you will have as the years go by.

There's no foundation to build on. No long term trusted relationships. Everyone is forming early impressions about you. You gather as many of your key people around you as possible to review the issue. But ultimately, the determination is yours. These decisions, quite often for both good and for bad, shape your tenure as president.

You may remember Colonel Nicholson, in the River Kwai. He is the perfectionist who builds an extraordinary bridge. There comes a time, however when he has to blow it up. He utters the famous line: "My god, what have I done?" There are times you may ask the same question.

"You need to look at all the issues," Jake Schrum says. "In the early days, they mount like towering mountains. You listen to everyone you possibly can. In the end you need to make some hard decisions. You own them.

"The decisions are easier if you keep remembering that students are what you are all about. That is your major focus. You want them to have a transformational experience. The decisions need to be made with that in mind."

Joseph White told me that when he went to the University of Illinois, he found an efficient and very well run institution. But there were some immediate decisions regarding staff that had to be made. His comments are particularly significant.

"I have had to fire a lot of people over the years. That was true even in those early days at the university. It's my least favorite part of my job, but it's necessary and I've always felt that I owe it to the people who are doing a good job. I do it clearly, cleanly, fairly, and personally.

"I've been struck by how often a person being fired for poor performance actually greets the news with relief. I think they probably know they had it coming."

I want you to particularly note what comes next from White.

"By the way, I've never met a leader who fired someone for poor performance who hasn't said, 'In retrospect, I wish I had done it sooner.'"

Scott Miller says it doesn't take much time to decide about the staff. "I know by the second day on campus, everyone will hit me. I have to be prepared for that. I listen as carefully as I possibly can and begin making some decisions about my senior staff."

It sometimes happens that some of your senior officers have to go. The final decision is the president's. It shouldn't take much time to make that determination. Follow Hillel's admonition, "If not now, when."

You have a window of opportunity to make some changes in the first few months. That's when the decision should be made.

After that, it becomes increasingly more difficult.

"But here's the problem," says Steve Jennings. "In those early months, you spend a lot of time putting out institutional fires. No matter how good the situation is at the college, there are always issues. That means you are making decisions, at times major decisions, in the first few months."

You may feel like you're constantly caught up in the thick of thin things. Like Steve Jennings, you are a one-person fire department, putting out fires and rescuing the college from dire circumstances. With all that's going on, you still must attend to the important decisions.

There are times when you have collected all the necessary data and have spoken with every possible relevant person. You're still not certain. Act like Carl Sandburg: "I am an idealist. I don't know where I'm going, but I'm on my way."

Let's say you are facing a difficult decision. Begin by leaving all old solutions behind. You want to break the iron frame of customs and traditions and forge the unknown and unexplored. Eschew an attachment to the time-honored ways. You should have a certain irreverence for established procedure.

Here are some good questions to ask.

1.   Do I have enough of the information I need?

2.   Is there any possible other person whose input could help move this forward for me?

3.   Is it quite clear that I am the person to make this decision?

4.   Have I looked at all the angles— can I come at this from a different perspective?

5. Am I hesitating because I want to defer or am afraid to make the decision?

Most of the time, you won't have all the empirical evidence you need. It continues to be a "yes, but…" or "but, what if…" Apply what Emerson called, "The blessed impulse."

It's what he referred to as the intuitive hunch, the vision that comes to you in a flash that it's the right thing to do. I find so often these blessed impulses help form the right decision.

Your wise and correct decision comes from combining whatever hard data you can acquire along with all the other information that is questionable or subjective. You mix the two generously with your intuitive proclivity. You will come out all right.

There's one thing more to remember. The board chose you because they feel you are precisely the right person. They have confidence in you. Trust your impulses. Make the decision.

I am reminded that you are free to decide. In fact, the decision is yours. But you are not free to choose the consequences of your decision. That's what makes it difficult.

Emerson's advice helps: "Always, always, always do what you are afraid to do." But it can be painful. There is a spiritual axiom that God never closes one door without opening another. But I find that sometimes the hallway in between is murder.

6

SEND THEM ON A CRUISE
(How to Deal with Your Predecessor)

I worked with John S. Bailey for the 30-plus years of his presidency at the college. He salvaged a moribund institution and built it into the largest private college in Europe. When he retired this year, he left the college with an endowment of over $230 million.

There is so much I admire about him. It could fill pages. What I'm going to tell you about here, in the scheme of things and all his achievements, is quite a small matter.

It was the way Jack paid reverence to all those he followed in office. There were two former presidents. They were invited to every special gathering, they had an honored place at graduation, and whenever they were in attendance at an event they were introduced with flourish. It was, "the striking of a great chord," as Ian Frazier once put it.

In the *Lord of the Rings,* there is that dramatic moment when Sam says of the ring, "Mr. Frodo, I can't carry it and its history for you, but I can carry you." That's Jack Bailey. He carried all his predecessors— with respect and tribute.

That was Bailey's style. He had the ego that could handle it. He also knew of the extraordinary regard and esteem in which he was held by the board, its students, and the entire Greek community. Every time he paid honor to the past, he actually enhanced his own presidency and honored the college.

Never insult an alligator until you have crossed the river. Some day in the future, you will cross that river yourself. Read what one of my presidents says about leaving office.

Mary Pat Seurkamp says that it's very important that you are respectful of the past. "No matter how you feel, no matter what kinds of questions are raised, respect your predecessor. Don't listen to the negative comments. Remember, there will come a time when you will have a successor!"

At times, it is difficult to honor the past. Especially if there have been some major bumps in the road and detours that led in the wrong direction. You can handle that. You are a strong president— self-confident, self-aware, control impulses, delay gratification, and are empathetic. You realize, also, your time will come.

Send them on a trip. That's Bruce Heilman's suggestion.

"It's a good idea for the predecessor to be away from the campus for 6 months or so. If there is a good relationship between the predecessor and the new president, be supportive of what they did, perhaps invite them to a board meeting or two, give them all the recognition you can. But make certain they are not involved with board members. They must not serve on the board. Perhaps a nice going away present for the past president is a 6 month cruise!"

All the presidents I spoke with agree that having your predecessor serve on the board is a serious mistake. He can serve as chancellor— and that should only be special recognition for a long and successful tenure.

"The only reason to have a retiring president as chancellor is if he is expected to raise funds for the college," says James Fisher. I would echo that. Or perhaps to help maintain some important relationships and build a bridge between the old and the new.

Very sticky business, this issue about naming your predecessor chancellor or having them serve on the board after his retirement. At Baylor University, the very successful and popular president was asked to serve on the board. He accepted. He was also named chancellor and had an office on the campus.

It became a very difficult situation for the new president. Impossible in some ways.

The newly named chancellor kept in regular contact with board members— he loved it. They kept in contact with him. When it came time for really significant decisions, as a board member, he took a vocal and strong position. Sometimes this was in direct opposition to what the new president was advocating.

I remember one board meeting when he was diametrically opposed to the recommendation of the president. His voice rose. He pounded the table. At this point, it's appropriate to quote from Milton's *Paradise Lost:* "All hell broke loose."

Bruce Heilman has bridged that problem. At the University of Richmond, he was named chancellor after an extremely successful presidency— and has served four presidents since. He also continues to be the major fundraiser on the campus. He understands that fundraising is his only responsibility— that and being a roaring advocate for the president.

Jim Fisher agrees: "The only possible reason for keeping the past president on is for fundraising. If they are not going to do that, what is the rationale?"

There's even a great danger of having them on the campus. There's the tendency of some of the faculty, and even the senior officers, to want to visit with the former president. These too often are more gripe or gossip sessions than social.

If the former president has been a fundraising whiz, there may be reason for keeping her on as chancellor. But trustees do not do the institution or the new president a favor by giving the title of chancellor to the former president if there aren't specific functions and objectives. Make it clear this is done in complete accordance with the new president, agreed upon in advance.

For the new president, it must not be a surprise in finding out your first day you have the former president on your doorstep.

It can become a delicate and difficult situation. Let's say the board has completed most of the interviewing. The Selection Committee is now down to its last two candidates. Both candidates keenly want the position. Moving to a presidency has been part of their dreams for years.

I'll tell you what can happen. I was at a meeting of a Selection Committee when they were interviewing one of the two final candidates. He was their first choice. *Primus enter pares*— first among equals. Here's how the discussion went.

"We've had a really good eight-year run with our president. He's done a great deal for the college. We've decided to keep him on as chancellor. We hope you feel all right about that."

As soon as I heard that comment, I looked at the candidate. The fist clenched, the jaw tightened, he cleared his throat two or three times. I was listening with my eyes.

There was a long pause. He was experiencing the silence of a Trappis Monk. Finally, he spoke.

"Well…well certainly. I'm sure we'll be able to work well together. Did you have something specific in mind he would be doing?"

"No, not really. We thought you two would figure out what was best for the college. We knew you could work it out."

What would you have done? Is this the issue on which you would have made it a *make or break* decision for the board. Remember, the candidate really wanted the job. It was a perfect situation for him.

Nothing more was said. This candidate was selected. As it worked out, it turned into a great working relationship between the two of them. But that is not always the case. It doesn't always work out that way. There are times the relationship makes the winds rise and the white-caps swell.

The chancellor, the former president, should not report to the board. She should be a direct report to the president. Having this person as chancellor should be a plus, or at the very least a neutral. If it's any less than that, it's not worth it. The juice isn't worth the squeeze.

Keeping the former president on in some capacity should not be the kind of decision you have to make. That's like getting between a dog and a lamppost. That should be a function of the chairman of the board, but in total agreement with you.

I remember what happened at Westminster Choir College (Princeton, New Jersey— now a part of Rider University), some years ago. John Finley Williamson was the revered founder of the college. He led it to remarkable acclaim and an astounding reputation. After 30 years or so, it was time for him to retire.

(I have a theory, not at all substantiated by empirical evidence. Ralph Waldo Emerson said, "An institution is the lengthened shadow of one person." This can too often be the case, especially with a founder.

It seems to me that when you have a president who has been extremely successful and enjoys near-venerable admiration and affection from all of the college community— it is often best to appoint an interim president for a year. This helps measurably to make the bridge from the old to the new.)

Following John Finley Williamson, the new president had an extraordinary challenge. He combined this with a bulging ego.

It was his decision not to invite Williamson back for any events. Worse than that, it was common knowledge he would not allow Williamson to return to the campus for any reason at all.

Bad decision! The new president was gone a year later.

When Lee Hastings Bristol, Jr. was then selected as the next president, the first thing he did was invite Williamson back to the campus. There were several thousand people gathered to greet him. The ovation went on forever, uninterrupted. Bristol became an immediate hero.

James Johnson had an even more difficult situation he faced. The former president had been at the college for 20 years, the last seven as president. The president's wife was called, "the First Lady." (You're beginning to get the picture.) She was on the payroll and had an office next to Johnson's.

The second day in office, she asked Johnson if she could stay on the payroll and keep her office. He told her she could not. That should have been a discussion the board had with the former president and "the First Lady" before the arrival of the new president. Johnson should not have had to deal with that. Guess who becomes the bad guy.

Thomas Aquinas College is nestled in a valley surrounded by beautiful mountains. It's what Ronald Reagan said about his ranch— "I don't know if this is heaven, but it has the same zip code." The college is only 30 years old.

Its founder was the spirit and inspiration that made it happen. Thomas Aquinas would not have been possible without him.

Giving birth and being able to sustain the operation are two different things. It doesn't follow, in fact it seldom does— that the qualities necessary in bringing about the birth of an institution can be transferred effectively to maintaining its operation. This was certainly the situation at Thomas Aquinas.

The founder was the president since its first days, and now the college was close to bankruptcy. Thomas Dillon's immediate task was to get the college out of significant debt, stabilize it, and then advance it forward. His focus was riveted on this.

"I was dean of the college in my late 20s. I was still quite young when I became president. Being a dean is one thing. Taking over the presidency is an entirely different matter. It's awesome. Even in the first few days, I was overwhelmed by the experience. But I had fire in my belly for the college— and that made everything possible.

Out of deep respect for the founder, the board somehow decided to keep him involved. They elected him a trustee. Not good.

Maria Grant is chair of the Thomas Aquinas board. She tells me of a very difficult situation.

"We had a decision, a major one, that came up last year. The board was somewhat divided but weighing heavily on behalf of the president's position. The founder was diametrically opposed and was outspoken about it. He was living in the past, bounded to nostalgia and old ways of doing things.

"Dillon's position was absolutely right. He finally won the vote. But not before an agonizing and traumatic session."

Stephen Jennings tells another frightening story. This is his fourth time around and understands a good bit about being an effective leader. He knows better now about having a prior understanding with the board regarding his predecessor.

"In one of my presidencies, the former president stuck around so long they finally had to carry him out." I challenged him.

"You mean they had to ask him to leave?"

"No, I mean they had to carry him out, literally."

The former president had had a stroke. He didn't want to quit. He was several years beyond the time of his effectiveness. Even though he could not function, he was brought to his office on the executive floor every day.

In a very kind and thoughtful way, the board should have helped the former president understand that his continuing to come to the office and just sit wasn't helping the college he so loved. But the board didn't take action. They didn't want to hurt his feelings. Jennings had a difficult decision he had to face. He finally had to force the situation.

Many presidents, near or at the end of their careers, seem unaware of the dangers of staying on too long. But they find leaving extremely difficult. Some are willing to step down in name, but not in fact.

Some of these outstanding, grand old presidents act like they will be the exception. They are not. Whatever their state of effectiveness. No matter how distinguished their tenure. They should not be asked to serve on the board. Period!

Listen to Scott Miller on the matter. You can count on him for his wisdom. He represents what Rossetti wrote: "I've been here before." This is Scott's third presidency. He is also a frequent writer on trusteeship.

"Having the former president on the board is terrible. Unacceptable. You may want to give the person the title of chancellor, but unless they have a specific function I wouldn't do even that and I wouldn't have them around.

"As a matter of fact, I think it's a good idea if the former president takes off for the year and is not anywhere close to the campus. That will give the new president the break that is necessary."

Bruce Heilman agrees. He believes the former president should not be on the campus in the early months.

"It's a good idea for the predecessor to be away from the campus for 6 months or so. Perhaps take a trip. The new president has all he can handle just to put his own imprint on the presidency. You don't want the former president getting in the way. Even if he works hard to dissolve into the background and not interfere, he is a presence."

It often works out best to be direct. This is what Lisa Marsh Ryerson did.

"My predecessor was one of my closest friends. He was my model and hero."

The former president was Lisa's mentor. He was an ideal leader. With him, Lisa felt like an acolyte in the wake of a priest.

"He knew me as a Dean of Students and then advanced me to Vice President and then to Executive Vice President. Everything I am, I owe to him.

"On my first day, I walked into his old office, now my new office. It was totally clean, not a single reminder of his presence. I quite soon noticed, however, that he had taken the office next to mine.

"I knew I had to have an honest talk with him. I felt we cared about each other enough he'd understand. I told him he should move off the campus. He understood entirely. And that's what he did. It would have been unacceptable to have him on the campus."

The truth is, it's much easier following a president who has not done a particularly good job. Perhaps even one who was told it was time to leave.

But what do you do about a retiring president who is greatly admired— but having trouble letting go? It can be a painful experience. They feel they are passing on to someone else a place they've put their indelible mark on.

For the highly esteemed president, letting go of such a substantial part of one's life can be emotionally intense. It can be comparable to giving your daughter away in marriage ("Who's that scoundrel she is running off with!").

For some who retire, they worry that their life will be like an old, cracked plate— one that's kept around in the pantry, but never brought out in proper company. In *Lord of the Rings*, there's that scene when Pippin thinks he's going to die and he says to Gandalf: "I didn't think it would end this way." That's how some feel.

Here are some general rules for you to follow.

1. Honor the past. Remember, you will have a successor someday. Often, the person you are replacing is now spare and unadorned— like a tree in late autumn, stripped of its leaves. Think of your predecessor (whether great, good, or otherwise) as a member of the same hallowed club. Much as Henry V said in his St. Crispin's day speech: "We few, we happy few, we band of brothers."

I had one president tell me it was really difficult. Her predecessor had done a horrible job and after four unsuccessful years, was finally fired. The board waited too long before taking action. The president had been a college Wizard of Oz, but after four baneful years, the board finally pulled back the curtain.

"What do I say when someone speaks disparagingly about the past. Well, to begin with, Sue DeWine tells me, "I try to avoid the issue." I quickly bring up another subject.

"If I'm really drawn into it, I will simply say something such as, 'This is such a great institution with a wonderful past. I'm so proud to be leading the college and I hope I'll be worthy of the honor.'

"And one thing I'm adamant about. I'm never negative at a board meeting about the past. I want trustees to focus on the future."

On this last point, I think trustees are aware of the president who is both self-righteous and unforgiving of others. Even when you're asked about the past, you will find that in many situations, it shows great command of your language to say nothing.

The Spanish say: *En Boca Cerrada No Entran Moscas*— if you keep your mouth shut, the flies won't get in.

2. If the former president stays in the community or ends up on the campus on a regular basis, you may have a situation you need to deal with. I worked with one college where the former president popped into his old office on a regular basis. Unannounced.

His former administrative assistant didn't know how to handle it, and couldn't. She didn't, after all, want to offend her former boss. They ended up chatting while the clock ticked on.

The new president felt a bit like Vito Corleone when he sat

down with the Five Families and said: "How did it come to this?" The president had to deal with it.

If it's at all comfortable, and you have a situation like this, you may wish to have a frank and thoughtful talk with your predecessor. That's what happened in the case of the college I just wrote about. And it worked out well.

If it's uncomfortable or if the situation continues, you should talk with the chairman of your board. There are times when it is best not to get in the middle of something like this— as they say, between the firing squad and the victim.

3. The chair of the board should have a very clear understanding with the new president about the role of the predecessor. I like to have this specific and in writing. I want to make certain the former president, also, has a copy.

This way there is nothing left to chance. No ambiguity. The chair is even allowed to say to your predecessor that it might be best if he is not around the campus for the next three or four months other than the transition between the two of you and the Inauguration.

4. I was at a meeting of the board when the acceptance of the new president was announced. Most trustees had met her and they were delighted with the selection. It was decided that there would be a six-month period of transition, the old to the new.

It sent shivers through me. I believe that long a transition is absolutely unnecessary. I explained to the board why I felt this way. It's impossible that it requires that much time to impart information. Further, there is a tendency to keep bumping into each other. It is certainly not a favor to the new president.

It's what Chekhov said— that the end still seems far off, and is immensely complicated and difficult, and it often appears only just the beginning.

The new president is eager to start. To put her own imprint on the presidency. It's what Frank Sinatra sang: "I'll do it my way."

There's another issue. The former president may not have the right perspective, or may be too wedded to the old. Buddha may have been thinking of this exact situation. Read what he said:

"Do not always believe what you hear. Do not necessarily believe in past authority, your elders, or those who go before you. Do not believe in tradition simply because it is handed down over the years. But after carefully observation and analysis, when it agrees with reason and what you believe, and it will benefit one and all, then accept it and live by it."

Scott Miller says he likes to have three or four hours with his predecessor. Maybe even a full day or two. But in that time he is able to absorb everything that is necessary. From that point on, he gains his information by talking to others, probing, and listening.

Some former presidents remain vibrant, innovative, and open to new ideas. This can be helpful in the transition. But I find some, to use the words of James Salter, "where the fire has died, the ashes are cold— very sad, worn, hollow, like the remains of an old oak."

You are a new president. You are a zealous evangelist for the college. You approach the mission with reverence, but with also an inquisitive mind. You examine everything.

You are as curious and probing as you can be, and not afraid of a paradox or an outright contradiction in what you find. Hopefully all of this points the way to your exciting and productive future.

I suggest a quick transition, an appropriate bridge between the old and the new. And now you are on your own.

5. If the board decides to name your predecessor chancellor with an active role of some sort, be certain you find out in advance what the purpose of the position is. I prefer to have that spelled out before you take office.

The chancellor should report to you, not the board. I'll make that more emphatic: The chancellor must not report to the board.

Most often, the new chancellor is given the role of fundraising. The problem is that as president, he was not very adept at fundraising, or he never did any at all. All of a sudden, with the magic of a new title, the old is expected to turn into a fundraising wizard— something that he had never before been in all his years.

I don't believe people change. You can't teach an old rat to kiss a cat. It proves the axiom Joseph Conrad set down in *The Secret Agent:* "We never cease to be ourselves."

If the board does decide to name your predecessor the chancellor, it should have your approval and should be on a year-to-year contract. There should be specific objectives that are given to her and evaluated by you. You, and only you, make the decision about the renewal of the contract.

If your predecessor becomes chancellor, there should be a great flurry of activity by him. Unbounded loyalty to you. A willingness to do anything necessary.

Your new chancellor should rise and soar like an eagle. Instead, sadly, I find in too many situations there is a great flapping of wings and an inability to get off the ground.

6. I find in many situations, the former president is given an office. This happens often even if she is not named chancellor. This is frequently done when your predecessor has served a distinguished and long tenure. It's a way of paying tribute to her presidency.

I prefer to have the office off campus. If that doesn't work, have the office remote from yours and out of the way of traffic. It mustn't end up being a place where people go to gripe, gossip, or gibber of the wondrous past.

My strong preference is that having an office on the campus is to be avoided. I have the same feeling about this as I would about a circular saw striking a knot in the wood. You are never a safe distance from despair.

Whatever the board's decision regarding your predecessor, it should be cleared with you. It's not enough to make this a random or casual discussion. It needs to be very clear about the rationale, what is expected, and your true feelings. (Repeat: True feelings.)

You may agree completely with the board's decision. You believe the two of you will work well together— a perfect team. If you do agree, just remember St. Paul's admonition: "Bear all things, endure all things."

7. What I'm about to tell you next should be considered as irreproachable and unimpeachable as the Pope's Encyclical to his Bishops. Your predecessor should not be a member of the Board. And under only the most unusual circumstances should she be

invited to board meetings. This would be the exception.

In this regard, what I write is absolutely clear to me. I feel like the Apostle Paul when he wrote to the Galetians: "What I tell you is the plain and perfect truth."

8. And finally, in dealing with your predecessor, if things become difficult or sensitive, follow the same wisdom you would employ in Whitewater Rafting:

- Whitewater (being president) is what you came for. Have fun and enjoy it.

- Rest at all the calm places— there will be more whitewater soon.

- Never stop paddling, even when it seems hopeless. It's your only hope if you get into trouble.

- Do not panic.

- If you go under, remain calm, think carefully about your situation, and let go of everything. Eventually you *will* come back up.

7

THE MAGIC
PARTNERSHIP
(Working with the Board)

When the chairman of your board says: Don't worry about what other board members are saying about you— worry a lot about it. That's a good rule to follow.

In those early months, you can understand how board members can become frustrated and then disappointed if it appears you're not getting the job done. They can sense when you avoid making difficult decisions, or are not making any decisions at all.

Board members may start getting phone calls from alumni and donors. And faculty members have a way of contacting trustees (even though they are not supposed to). All of this can cause early and serious issues.

But worst of all is when the board senses in the early months of your presidency that the institution seems to be adrift, rudderless.

Actually, I find in many cases the problem isn't that the board expects too much. It's that they expect too little. Excellence always causes a problem for those who are willing to settle for mediocrity.

There's probably no one in the nation who is a greater authority on trusteeship than James Fisher. As they say, he has written the books— and they should be required reading for you.

He says that it is absolutely essential in the early days that you begin bonding with board members, particularly the chair. He admonishes that it should occupy a major part of your time the first three or four weeks. It's that important.

"Make certain," Fisher says, "that the board establishes their objectives for the new president before he or she ever arrives. It's important that trustees have a full understanding and agreement of what they expect from the new president."

When these objectives are in place, they need to be presented to the new president. If you don't know what is expected, how will you know how you are doing? How can you be evaluated? What is most desirable is that the Board's vision and hopes need to be carefully reviewed by the new president and negotiated if necessary at the time of engagement.

Fisher makes another point. This time with even greater emphasis. (He always makes his points with great emphasis!) I challenged him on it. Then I thought about it some more and I suspect he's quite right.

"I believe that no college or university has reached its highest attainment and considered to be among the most outstanding in its class because of the chair of the board or the trustees. That's true no matter how significant a role the chair or the board has played.

"The institution is the shadow of the president. There are no exceptions. Period."

I have seen some situations where the chair played such a prominent role that he has dominated and magnified the momentum and progress of the college. Or working closely with the president, the two of them have acted as one. These are exceptions.

Tom Peters agrees with Fisher. He says: "Nothing significant in this world happens except at the initiative of a single person." That's true. That's where it starts. That's you. It begins with you, the new president.

I would add to Fisher's statement something I feel keenly about. I believe the president, no matter how qualified, no matter how effective, no matter how strong a leader— cannot take the institution beyond the level of the board. It takes the two, working in a very close bond that creates the kind of synergy that propels a good institution into a great college.

I call it a *Magic Partnership* when that happens. Both the board and the president are locked in a dance of spirit, hope, and vision— and neither can break the other's embrace.

Richard Jewell joined his college's board when he was 29— the youngest in the history of Grove City College. He served on that board for the next 25 years. (Rotation was a word mentioned in only reverent whispers around the college— in hushed tones, as a priest might speak to the Holy Father.)

He told me what it was like in board meetings when he first

became a trustee. The board met only twice a year. The meetings lasted only for lunch and a few minutes beyond that. The only decision a trustee had to make was: Do you want fish or meat?

The treasurer would get up at the meeting and say something like: "We're in the black." There would be a pause and some constrained applause. The head of the Investment Committee would then get up and say: "We made money this year." Again, quiet applause. Then the meeting would end.

Because he knew the college so well, Jewell hit the ground running when he was elected president. He knew most of the senior officers and had great confidence in them.

When he became president, he wasn't surprised at how little the board actually knew about the college. He was certain there had to be a change in the governing culture. He considered this of priority importance.

Dick wants his board members to bring passion, wealth, and wisdom. As Tennyson wrote, "Strong in will, to strive, to seek, to dare— and not to yield." Dick has really worked at that.

I feel a board should feel the future never looked brighter. They should also understand the challenges never were as complex. Any trustee who isn't exhilarated by both of these statements may be too tired to be much use on the board.

Grove City College now has a superb board, totally engaged. Each member meets Jewell's three criteria: Passion. Wealth. Wisdom.

It was a split vote when Dick was elected president. There were some who felt that because he did not have direct experience in higher education, he did not have the necessary qualifications. Nor did he have a doctorate.

For those reasons, he made it his business to visit every single trustee, both his pros and the cons, in the first few weeks after he took office. He did this even though he knew them all very well. He continues to be in contact with his trustees on a monthly basis— by personal visits and by telephone.

He has some excellent advice to offer. Try to find out why you were chosen and what made the difference in your selection.

"I would caution new presidents to know all of the problems of the college before they take office, and determine as best they can the status of the school in all of the vital areas. Most important, they need to find out why they were chosen. Then, the new president needs to commit his unyielding resolve to make the changes that are necessary."

Let's take your situation for example. There was a large applicant pool. There must have been close to 100 seekers for the position. The board narrowed down the large pool to a short list of candidates. You were finally selected because of some very specific qualities and skills you brought to the table. It's important for you to know what these were.

It's perfectly all right to ask. I'll tell you how easy it is. Try something like this.

"I'm delighted to be with you and I really look forward to beginning what I hope will be a long tenure. I'm curious about something. If it seems appropriate, I would like to ask why I was chosen over other candidates. What was there in my background you felt was most important for the school at this time."

The process of the engagement doesn't always happen in an organized fashion. Take Ohio Valley University, for instance.

James Johnson received an emergency phone call Thanksgiving Day. He was elected in October and was supposed to begin his presidency in June. That gave him plenty of time to clear his office of unfinished work, get settled, and do the kind of advance work he knew was necessary before taking office.

But in the last week in November, seven months before he was to begin his new post, the chairman of the board called. They wanted him right away.

"James, we need you. We need you now." James went.

"The board felt there were some serious problems, but they didn't know what the problems were. Nothing was working. There wasn't enough money to make payroll in the summer. They wondered if they would have to close the school. They felt they needed me right away to help solve some of those issues.

"I walked into a situation that was in total disarray. It was a broken college. As soon as I got there, I put a spending freeze into effect.

"I'll tell you how bad the situation was. When I looked around my office for a wastebasket, there wasn't one. When I asked, the finance office to order a wastebasket for me, they told me there wasn't enough money to buy one.

"I spent my early days meeting with every trustee. I wanted to have more time on the campus but I felt the board was my priority. I knew that in order to succeed, we needed a totally committed board.

"After my individual visits, we had an early emergency meeting of the board. I gave them hope. I told them I could save the college, but I couldn't do it without their help. They gave me their commitment.

"I believe my most important act with the board was— I gave them hope."

Scott Miller says the very best time to ask for a commitment from the board is very early in your tenure. "I knew we had a serious financial problem. In the very first month, at a board meeting, I asked trustees for a $50 million commitment.

"They were shocked. But I also think they were absolutely delighted. At last, they felt they could make a difference. No one had pressed them before. (I imagine at this point, Scott Miller broke out in a silent rendition of the Doxology.)

"When I called on board members in that first month, I let them know how critically important their participation was. I asked for help in ongoing giving, endowment, and their estate plans. I let them know I couldn't do it without their help."

The board is most receptive to your requests in your early days. They will want to do whatever is necessary to make yours a successful venture. St. Francis of Assissi said to preach the Gospel to everyone and if necessary, use words that inflame.

Talk with your board about the resources you require in order to ensure the maximum effectiveness in your work. Ultimately, this means providing the funding necessary to meet the mission of the college.

These requests aren't limited to people and annual funds— although these are essential. Talk with them about what you need in facilities, equipment, grounds, technical support, and the right people in senior positions.

Most of all, you need encouragement and support from the board. You want the authority (you have it already by virtue of your position) and their endorsement to make tough decisions. They need to know this isn't a battle you fight on your own.

But nothing happens unless you first see the dream. You dream. You dare. You pass it on. "Pass it on," wrote Camus. "Just pass it on."

Lisa Ryerson knew all of the board members when she was elected president. She had come up through the ranks at Wells College— as an undergraduate, a dean of students, vice president, and then executive vice president. She felt that was all the more reason the board had to understand her new role and theirs. She didn't want them remembering her as the dean of students, or even as the executive vice president.

"In the early days, I made it clear who was governing and who was president. I thought that was terribly important. You certainly don't keep arm's length from the board, and you want them knowing as much as possible about what is going on at the College.

"But I don't want the trustees managing. I began visiting board members in the first few weeks. Even those I knew well and was very close to. I was on the road immediately. A close working relationship with the board is essential."

Esther Barrazone believes she pretty much knew all of the problems of the college when she took on the job. The board was quite clear with her. They were in a crisis situation. They held back nothing.

They had not met their budget in years. They were pilfering their endowment. Admissions were down, faculty spirits were low, trustees were bailing, there were talks of merging or going out of business. The problems and rumors were running wild, like flood water through a cracked dike.

"They seemed to know all the problems. But they didn't know what to do about them. In the end, they were wonderfully cooperative in working with me and about turning everything over. They helped in every way possible, but didn't get in my way.

"They understood clearly their role and mine. They determine policy. I execute.

"We had a frightful financial crisis and the board wasn't able to wrap its arms around it. Before I came, they figured they could still stay open as long as three years before they drew down all of their endowment. Actually, the endowment was almost all gone. They didn't really have much hope.

"Here's how serious it was. They took a vote. They had decided that if the college went out of business, and they expected it would, they would give whatever was left of their endowment to establish a foundation for the education of women.

"The good news is that they never had to go into debt for annual operations. The bad news is they achieved that by spending down their unrestricted endowment, year after year.

"They also told me there was a good possibility I would be the last president of the college. They really said that! They were quite clear about it. That's how desperate it was. They knew they had to do something dramatic and they wanted an entrepreneurial president.

"I look back and wonder whether I was totally sane when I took the job!

"In the first month, I knew what had to be done. The board allowed me to introduce a graduate program. It was the first time in our history we allowed men to enroll, but only as graduate students. One of my faculty members stopped me in the hall one day and said: 'I don't know what's more horrifying— seeing women in gym pants or men lined up in the old Ladie's Room.'

"When I came, the board was distressed and of low spirit. I had to convince them that they were actually not part of the problem. I had to give them hope. They simply hadn't had the kind of leadership they needed in order to become effective supporters and advocates.

"In my first few months, I had to determine what assignments I could give the board in order to effect a change. The problem was I had no free time to just think. I was entirely consumed in stopping the bleeding. I undertook massive cuts. I was working with faculty and moving around as fast as I possibly could."

If there has been a failed presidency before you arrive, the chances are good that the board has become far more involved in the operations and management of the college then is proper or desirable. Their involvement isn't totally surprising. They were simply filling a void.

Now is the time for correction. The board must understand that they do not ask *how* things are done. They ask *why* things are done. It's the boards job to see that the right things are done. It's the president's job to see that things are done right.

You have heard it said that the responsibility of the board is to hire and fire the president, and determine policy. Well, that's all true— but not quite that simple.

It is indeed the board's responsibility to hire and regularly and carefully evaluate the work of the president. And, yes, it determines policy. When that is done, trustees leave it up to the president and her staff to execute the policy.

It's the evaluation of the president that is a major issue. That should be done at least once a year.

In the new president's first year— the evaluation should be made after the first six months. That is something the chair will likely not think about. You may need to prompt her. It's important because if there needs to be a course correction, it should be done as early as possible.

There's one other responsibility that never seems to be mentioned. In importance, I think it ranks right behind the election of the president. It is the board's responsibility not to allow a deficit. And I don't speak of a financial deficit.

Let's say your college has been running a deficit. Or you're walking the financial tightrope— you can make it, or plunge, often without a safety net.

Actually, it's relatively easy for a board to give oversight to the management of a financial deficit. That's the wrong way.

They cut staff and faculty where they can. They put off necessary maintenance, cut services, delete some activities and courses, and let the property pretty much take care of itself. They don't increase salaries.

Bingo. They have managed to balance the budget.

But what trustees have created is a *Mission Deficit*. This is the most critical and dangerous of all. Because of all the cuts, they have not met the college's mission.

It is the board's responsibility to not allow a *Mission Deficit*. To permit this to happen is to compromise their trusteeship.

If there is a gap between the revenue the college is generating and what is required to meet its primary objective and mission, it is the board's responsibility to provide funds to close the gap. History will not deal kindly with a board that watches from the sidelines as the college goes adrift.

I call that the seagull practice of trusteeship. That's where men and women gather together, squawk a lot, flap their wings— and then fly away.

I love the word *trustees*. It implies a certain trust which has been passed on to a select group of men and women. This hand-picked group is pledged to ensure the well-being and vitality of the college. Board members hold in trust the future of the college. It is a covenant they make. They should not take that lightly.

It was a dire situation when Jake Schrum took over his first presidency. It was at Texas Wesleyan.

"There was a bonfire everywhere I looked. They had been in the red for 16 years. I'll tell you how bad the financial situation was. When I wanted to have a dinner for my first meeting with the board, I had to have a special campaign to raise the money.

"When I went there, it was on split vote. The board was divided about bringing me in as president. That meant I had a great deal to make up with those who voted against me. That very first week, I visited all board members. I think that's essential whether there's a split vote or not.

"I needed to define my vision and dreams for the college right away. I wasn't certain that all of the board understood where we were going and where we ought to be going. It was important that we all travel the same road together.

"Here's what makes it so important to visit board members. I asked questions and I listened.

"I wanted to know what has been the most positive moment for them at the college. What is their greatest concern? How should I be spending my time. What can I count on them to do for the college."

In the first few weeks after Bruce Heilman became president, he had a pretty good idea of what needed to be done. He went to visit every trustee in their home or in their office. He told them about his vision for the future. He made it clear he needed them and what was expected.

"In the first few days, I carefully examined the board roster. I wanted to see who was attending meetings, who was giving and how much, and who was bringing their friends to the institution. I told every trustee, every single one: 'I want you to give the university your first priority.'

"There is nothing more important to the success of a college than having an effective board. The recruiting cannot be successful if it's not done with the support, encouragement, and priority of the president. It starts with the president having a thorough understanding of the importance of trustees and the significant role they can play."

"I made it clear to the board that I wasn't employed to operate the institution. I was recruited to advance the institution.

That's an important distinction. The reason you must have that kind of a discussion with trustees is that you want them to know the college's success begins with the board.

"I told them I would provide the vision. I made it clear that I couldn't succeed without their help. If I'm not advancing the college with their help, we're standing still. All new presidents need to say to their boards, 'I work for you, but I can't do it without you. I need you.'

"I want new presidents to understand that they need the kind of board that others strive to be on. There needs to be a certain caché to being on the college board.

"Let them know you need their advice and counsel, their participation and involvement. Let them know that it's the only way you can be an effective president. It takes the board's total commitment and participation. You want your board to feel they are involved in a noble cause."

Dostoevsky writes, "You can't get along without us." Like a lightbulb to a moth. You, as a new president, can't succeed without a zealous and committed board, totally devoted to the college's growth and development.

It's all right to let the board know in those early days how you feel about certain things. When Heilman first became president, the board offered him a Pinto automobile.

"I told them I'm not going to be an economy president. I don't want an economy car. I certainly don't want the most expensive car, but I do want something that gives the impression of success. I can't be driving donors around in a Pinto." He ended up in a Buick.

Here is what often happens. The selection committee and the

board work very hard to match the new president to the college's perceived needs and problems. They want it to be a happy marriage. At the same time, there are some enormous concerns that have to be faced.

The reason you were selected was very likely that the board felt you could meet the troubling issues of the college at this given time in its history. You were the perfect choice.

The new president very often differs significantly from the person he or she succeeds. By the way, that is most often what is appropriate and needed. But the change in style and tempo can cause friction with some of the staff and with some of the board.

Mary Pat Seurkamp walked into precisely that sort of situation. "I was the first lay president in the history of the college. That meant there were many obstacles to overcome.

"My choice was not a popular one for every trustee. As a matter of fact, the board was split. It actually ended up that after the vote, some of the trustees were so upset they were not speaking to one another.

"I felt my first responsibility in those early days was to heal the wounds. Some of the board members quit, and I wanted them back. Eventually they returned. When I started, I had to move exceedingly fast. I called on all trustees in my first few weeks. Those who stayed and those who resigned."

Having an exceedingly strong board paves the road for your success as a president. It also determines the future of the college. A strong, dedicated board ensures the college's destiny.

Underline what comes next. You are responsible for the quality of the board. You are the coach.

There can be a serious problem inherent in the group that does the nominating of new board members. The committee members almost never select anyone above their own level of influence and affluence. Too often, I find they perpetuate their own mediocrity. And that contributes to having a mediocre board.

Here's what is essential to keep in mind. You don't elect board members. You select them. You, as the president, need to be at every meeting with the group that makes the selection of new board members. You need to make certain the committee aims high.

Not every board member needs to be nominated for another term. If they haven't been pulling their weight (giving, getting, attending meetings), send them on their way. The future of the college is too precious a trust to allow a non-producer to serve another term.

I've done away with the term, *Nominating Committee*. Eliminated it from my client's bylaws and lexicon. The term conjures up a group that meets once a year, maybe twice, to nominate trustees.

I believe so firmly that having the proper board is the future of the college that I insist with my clients that this is a committee that should meet four times a year. Better still— six. Meet by conference call or online, if necessary. Or think about Skype or "Go to Meetings.com".

Think about it. This is the committee that ultimately determines the college's future. For greatness…or otherwise. It is the most important committee of your board.

Stretch. Aim High. Keep your sights soaring. Your standards and qualifications should be of towering proportions.

I find that trustees will stand on tip-toes if the bar is raised high. It was Groucho Marx who said: "I would never belong to a club who would have me as a member." (I have a suggested Letter of Agreement in the Appendix that ensures a productive relationship.)

I change the name from Nominating to: *The Committee on Trusteeship*. That gives it the status and relevance it deserves.

The president meets with the committee. You are the coach. (I've never understood why some colleges will not have their president meet with the committee. That's like the New York Philharmonic without a conductor.)

In selecting new board members, you look for men and women with the 5-Ws.

1. *Work*. Willing to roll up their sleeves and get into the fray.

2. *Wisdom*. Able to make wise business decisions and use good judgment.

3. *Wealth*. Willing to contribute significantly (make the college one of their major philanthropies) and ask others to give.

4. *Wallop*. Have influence.

5. *Women*. Women now hold 57 percent of the net worth in this country. It will continue to grow. You better have strong representation.

I met some time ago with the Committee on Trusteeship at Scripps College (California). One of the board members said: "I think Jim Gamble (Proctor & Gamble) would make an excellent board member." Another board member said: "He'd never accept.

Don't even bother to ask."

The following year, Jim Gamble's name came up again. That same board member said: "I told you before. He'd never accept."

Following that meeting, the chair of the committee did indeed ask Jim to become a trustee. Gamble said he was honored but couldn't take it on at this time. Ask him again, he said.

When that was reported, I said to the Committee: "He's just putting you off. You'll likely never get him as a board member."

The following year Jim Gamble was asked again to be a board member. He accepted. He has contributed mightily over the years with his commitment and his dollars. (So much for the wise advice of a consultant!)

I have a very important suggestion for new presidents. I want this to be your credo. Please remember it in all you do— in seeking a person for your board (but also in soliciting a gift, in going after a top faculty member, or whatever), *You will be hurt more by those who would have said 'yes' but were not asked— than by those who say 'no.'*

Now, I ask you! Have you ever had your board compared to a flock of geese? Probably not. Let me explain.

When a goose flaps its wings, it creates an "uplift" for the bird following. By flying in a V formation, the whole flock adds 71 percent more to its flying range than if each bird flew alone.

LESSON: When the president and board members share a common purpose, commitment, and passion for the college, they can get where they are going quicker and more successfully because they are traveling on the thrust of one another.

If a goose falls out of formation, it suddenly feels the drag and resistance of trying to fly alone. It quickly gets back into formation to take advantage of the "lifting power" of the birds immediately in front.

LESSON: The president and trustees understand that it is important to follow those who have the proper direction and focus.

When the lead goose gets tired, it rotates back into the formation. Another bird takes its place at the point position.

LESSON: The president and trustees understand that it pays to take turns doing the hard tasks and sharing leadership. Even the lead goose knows it needs help at times.

The geese in formation honk from behind to encourage those up front to keep up their speed.

LESSON: Trustees need to make certain they are "honking" from behind to encourage and empower others.

When a goose gets sick or wounded or shot down, two geese drop out of formation and follow it down to help and give protection. They stay with the goose until it is able to fly again. Then they launch out on their own and catch up with the flock.

LESSON: If the president and trustees follow the good example of the geese, they stand by each other— through the most difficult of situations and trying of times. There is magic when the president and trustees work closely together for the success of the college.

Here endth the lesson.

8

Flying Like an Eagle
(A Senior Staff with Spirit and Commitment)

If you want to build a crack track team to win the high jump, you find some people who can jump seven feet, not seven people who can jump one foot. Let that be the lesson regarding your senior staff.

Here's what makes your task so difficult. You are going to have to make some careful evaluations in the first 120 days to make certain you have the right people in your senior positions. This becomes some of the most agonizing decisions you make in your early months.

The key is to be both systematic and strategic in your team-building of the senior staff. But also to be resolutely objective. That's what makes it most difficult.

It almost always happens. There will be those who are borderline who you want to save. And there are those who are borderline you feel you can help improve with the right coaching. You cross your fingers and hope they will grow like baked bread with triple yeast.

Then there are those you feel it is too early in your tenure to replace. Worse still, there are those where you feel you don't have enough time to replace, or you won't be able to find anyone better.

Your decision is very likely wrong in every case.

If you settle for a middling staff and middling ideas, you will always get run-of-the-mill staff and ideas. You mustn't settle for adequate or average. Never let good enough be good enough.

Joseph Heller came close to the truth when he satirized the phrase in his novel, *Catch 22*. "Some men are born to mediocrity, others achieve mediocrity, and some have mediocrity thrust upon them."

"What do you look for in replacing a vice president for development?" an Indiana college president asked me.

"You should look for a man or woman with passion for the college," I replied. "Confidence in their ability to do the job, uncommon skill, a hunger to win, and a desire to do more than is expected."

(I call this last criterion, the "And Then Some" factor. Very successful staff do what is expected— and then some.)

Those same criteria can be pretty much a measure for all your senior people. You want your entire team to have an abiding belief in the college. That is what fuels enthusiasm. Enthusiasm explodes into passion. And passion fires the soul and ignites the spirit. You are the president. The team takes its cue from you.

I had very much this same discussion with all the presidents I visited. They told me about the difficult decisions that had to be made regarding senior staff. James Fisher says that in the early weeks, you must spend a great deal of time in meetings with your senior officers.

"You will know very soon those who are worthy of continued tenure and those who should be moved to another position or more likely, dismissed. You begin to wonder about some of the selections of your predecessor."

There is a saying that there are some presidents who separate the men from the boys— and then hire the boys.

David McCullough, two-time Pulitzer Prize winner, writes mostly about presidents and leaders. He says: "Truman wasn't afraid to have strong people around him that were more accomplished than he. He delighted in it. That's why he had the strongest and most effective cabinet since George Washington."

Fisher says that in the early days, there should be many discussions with your senior staff. You go to each of these meetings knowing your specific objectives. "You want the team to know immediately of your vision and your hopes for the future."

You have to have an outcome in mind. At these early meetings especially, you want to ask yourself in advance— "what is it I want to accomplish?" That is the very question to ask before every meeting you have: What is it we hope to accomplish at this meeting? If you don't have or know the answer— cancel the meeting and save the doughnuts.

You want the staff to begin thinking in the future tense. Very early you will let them know what you want to achieve, how soon, and where you want to take the college.

You want to infuse the staff with your own passion. Ignite the spark. As the Apostle Paul told Timothy: "Fan your flame." He was telling Timothy not to let the fire go out that's in you. Stay passionate about all you do. Stay enthusiastic about your dreams.

Mary Pat Seurkamp is sorry she put-off making a change in her staff. Here is what she tells me.

"I can look back now and feel strongly that one of the serious mistakes I made was not taking action regarding a senior officer, one of the most important positions on our staff. I knew it was wrong to delay the decision. I should have done something. I should have stood my ground and done what I knew in the end would be best for the college. I knew that right away. After a few months it became certain. It simply wasn't going to work."

As soon as Stephen Jennings went into one of his presidencies, he knew the CFO had to leave. He was certain he would not be able to do the job. Steve made the decision quickly and never looked back. The same was true of the Dean of Enrollment. He made that change with equal speed. Both of these positions are critical to the success of the college.

What did Jennings do with another position? The problem was the person wasn't bad enough that you could make a case for dismissal. But not good enough you should keep him. Those are the most difficult decisions of all.

The person just didn't have enough fire and drive. Jennings

saw that immediately. But he kept him on, hoping for the best. In the end, it didn't work out and he had to dismiss the person. He lost valuable time delaying the decision.

John Hood knew he was in trouble. "I went around to the offices of all of the senior officers. The offices were in shambles. It was so bad, I brought in a professional photographer to take photos.

"Then I called a meeting of the senior staff. I showed them the photos and I said they better do something about their offices. I asked, 'How can you operate an efficient and effective program if your office is a total mess.' I told them they had to maintain certain standards and one of those was a tidy office.

"This may seem like a small matter. Some will even think I was getting too involved in details. But in my judgment, Oxford has to stand for something. It has the world's highest academic standards. But anyone walking into that sort of a sloppy office would quickly minimize the importance of that officer and the significance of the university."

It didn't take long for Hood to realize that his number two person had to leave and the CFO wasn't pulling his weight. The decisions were made early, quickly, but with compassion. He told me it isn't fair to the rest of the senior staff that are doing a good job to have to carry the weight of those who aren't.

"I wanted to make certain, also, that my senior staff understood that they have a great future ahead of them instead of worrying about the past. It was all about new beginnings."

Go ahead. Make the decision.

Joseph White is former Head of the Business School at the

University of Michigan and Interim President there before he became president of the University of Illinois. He is considered a doyen on the topic of leadership. He has the credentials.

"I've never met a leader who had to fire someone for poor performance who hasn't said in retrospect: 'I wish I had done it sooner.'" That's what White tells me.

It's perfectly in order to be demanding (perhaps this is too strong a word). You quite soon discover one of your senior staff who sets low personal objectives— then consistently fails to achieve them.

But make certain you're not one of those who is never satisfied. You will destroy the spirit of your senior team.

You press your staff to make realistic commitments. Then you hold them to their promises. But if you're one of those who is never satisfied, you will just sap the motivation of your key people.

It's the job of the new president to establish specific expectations and objectives. You will find when you do this, the behavior of the staff quickly begins taking shape.

It's important to let your senior staff (and the faculty, too) know who you are, what you are about, and what you expect: "This is the way I do things. I hope this will help in your working with me. We can accomplish great things working together. But you need to know there are some things that drive me crazy. Here's how we can avoid some of those items…"

Here's a warning from Jake Schrum. "You need to know you have the right people in place. I found I had a real problem with the finance person and the head of admissions. Both are critical to the success of the college. I determined that right away. With the other members of the team, I felt they could get the job done.

"This was my first presidency. One of the mistakes I made, and I think this is true of a lot of first-time presidents, you want to wait until you find out whether a person can make it or not. You want to give them a little extra rope. You want to study the situation a little bit. The problem is, it never gets better. I'm convinced your first instincts are the best."

James Johnson had a bit different type of problem. "Things were in such desperate shape, I met with the senior staff every day I was on campus. I felt my job was to help build their spirits and morale.

"I did everything I could to give them hope. That was my mission— to give them hope. There was one situation I had to change immediately. I didn't fire the person, I moved him into a position where he was more adequately suited.

"But here was the problem. At every one of our meetings, I was told about all the things that couldn't be done. 'We tried that before.' 'It won't work here.' 'It's not in our budget.' They gave me an unending stream of reasons why things couldn't be done.

"I finally put my foot down. I told them I didn't want any more negative people on my staff. If anyone said they weren't able to do a job or used the word *can't*, I would be after them. I needed positive support and an optimistic staff."

I'm one with Johnson. Being a new president, success with the senior staff is sometimes a matter of not holding great cards but in playing very effectively the cards you are dealt. Like James, I eschew the word, *can't*. It is not in my vocabulary. It must not be in yours.

Georgia Nugent wishes she had done it sooner.

"When I came as a new president, there was one area that I really wasn't familiar with. But even not knowing much about it, I was pretty certain that the person was not right for the position. But I thought if I worked with her, I could help her become a stronger person.

"It didn't work. I put up with it for two years and then finally made the decision. She would have to leave. If I had it to do over again, I would have acted in the first few months. You know that you are going to have to do this. Just do it."

As Kenny Rogers tells us: "You gotta know when to hold 'em, know when to fold 'em, know when to walk away, and know when to run." He would have made a great consultant.

Two years is far too long to wait. Georgia recognizes that now. Think of how it impacted the college. Think of how it affected the rest of the senior staff who were doing a good job. Think of the loss to the president's success. Think of the hurt it caused to the ultimate beneficiaries of the college—the students. You will be measured on how quickly you can make these decisions.

It's not easy. The decisions are tough and can break you up. Ernest Hemingway said that the world breaks all of us and we grow stronger in all the broken places.

Ralph Waldo Emerson talks about listening to the inner voice and going with it— sometimes against all voices to the contrary. There is something indeed divine about the intuitive voice of yours.

One word of caution. It is, of course, possible to clean house precipitously. But it is far more common to keep people longer than wise. I heard it from everyone. There's always the feeling you can inspire a person to do a more effective job. This doesn't happen very often. Almost never.

It's easy to convince yourself of your ability to motivate. New presidents, especially those with a collegial style, want to give members of the senior staff a chance to prove themselves. You want to be fair.

You tell yourself: I can make these people be far more effective than my predecessor. Let's be honest. That's the truth of it. You say: "All it takes is hard work on my part, listening, giving plenty of support, and adding my powerful leadership."

There are times you have to forget the cheese. Just find a way to get out of the trap.

Keeping team members with a history of mediocre performance seldom works. Those early months are your honeymoon. If changes are necessary, that's the time to make them.

Being a college president takes patience, understanding, and implacable purpose. That is your lot. As they say, no pain, no gain. Critically important choices. Few easy decisions.

It's a perplexing conundrum, what to do. It must be what Sisyphus might have felt if one day his boulder stopped, rested on the hill top, and failed to roll back down.

You are the leader. You have been selected to improve the performance of the college in every aspect of its activity. To think of all the exciting possibilities for the college enters you into a magical progression. You are expected to bring new ideas and make tough decisions.

You're hoping to instill a "you can move faster than a speeding bullet" spirit of achievement among your key people. But you may discover that some on your senior staff are not sufficiently able or flexible enough to embrace change. You're flying like an eagle but at times, you find you are working with turkeys.

You establish authority, while at the same time encouraging input and consultation. And collaboration. It can be a difficult combination to balance. Their differing opinions ricochet around the room like bullets.

Your vice presidents and staff should feel free to express their ideas without concern, rebuke, or isolation. They may not see eye-to-eye with you on every issue. Do not emulate Churchill who said: "I totally believe in reasonable discussion provided it ends in compliance with my own views."

Your staff has a choice. They can either challenge you or remain silent. You have to create the right climate for discussion.

You may have some staff who agree with you and others who do not agree at all. Both are equally valuable. Objections are like a grindstone. They either grind you down or polish you up.

If the staff remains silent, they will be of no assistance to you. It's up to you to encourage stimulating challenge and ideas. A clash of thinking or an objection is not a disaster or a threat— it is an opportunity.

You shouldn't feel you need to build consensus around very difficult decisions. At times, that's your dilemma. If you always aim at consensus and won't make a decision until you do, that can get you into a great deal of trouble.

It's *analysis paralysis*. You will be accused of being intent on listening to everyone's counsel before making a decision. A fence-sitter with both ears to the ground.

Here's what you must do. You get as much input from the staff as you possibly can. You have your key people provide you with their thoughts and views. You ask for as much information as you possibly can. Then you make the decision. You let everyone know the final decision and the responsibility is ultimately yours.

It is obviously important to listen to all of your senior people. But in the end, you go with what you believe. That's why you were chosen to be president.

You meet very often in those early days with your senior staff. Some of the presidents I visited with had two or three meetings a week for the first several months. George Will says that football combines the two worst features of American life: violence and committee meetings.

I attended one senior staff meeting recently at a West Coast college. Everyone spoke about how busy they were. I told them not to confuse being busy with being productive. There's an important distinction.

"If the entire senior team spends the whole day pushing against Old Main on the campus, they won't move it. They have been busy, but they haven't been productive."

There will be times you will be frustrated. (Hopefully, this doesn't dominate your life as a new president.) You have done all you can to move your senior staff upward and forward.

You have motivated, cajoled, threatened, and have just come short of pleading. You are reminded of blades of grass that suffer whenever elephants gather together.

Here's the definition of *inertia*. In physics, it is the property of matter that causes objects to resist change in their direction or speed. That can sound like some of your staff. As Tony Soprano liked to say, "Whaddya gonna do?" Force must be therefore applied to make a change.

In physics, *momentum* is the fundamental quality that characterizes the motion of any object. If you want to be specific (for those of you who have a Ph.D. in physics), momentum is the product of the mass of a body multiplied by its velocity. (Are you still with me?) The larger the mass (read that, *inertia*), the greater the force that must be applied to get it to change direction or speed.

You may have members of the senior staff who are prisoners of their past procedures. A hardening of their aspirations. At times, you may have to grab them by the lapels and shake them. Among your staff, there must be determination, a commitment, and an unending desire to make great things happen.

What is most important and of critical necessity is that your senior staff join you in having a complete understanding of your vision for the college. They must have a passion for the college. What you want in your senior staff is a keenness trembling within them, like a pilot light on a gas stove.

They must be willing to focus and become involved in what matters most. The true business of the college—transforming the lives of its students.

At times, you may have to work against difficult odds.

Chances are, the traditions and practices of the past and the changes you seek that will be coming in the future, will force that. You understand full well that a staff that will never walk except in old tracks, will never make new discoveries.

It will mean that your senior staff has to hit targets that tax them, create new strategies, and think of innovative ways of doing things. They need to understand that under your leadership, they must never stop stretching, seeking, growing, and redefining themselves.

They need to know they are the glue that holds the college together. The senior staff make a commitment to do whatever is necessary for the good of the college. It all comes from having an intense focus on what is really imperative. The driving mission of the college and preparing young men and women for a fulfilling life into the future.

Remember to listen to your inner voice. Yours may have been whispering the same thing Joseph White heard from his.

"I knew on my very first meeting, I had the wrong person in one of our university's most significant position. I knew I had to make a change. In this case I couldn't do it immediately. But it didn't take very long before I made the change. In my early few months, I laid the groundwork for the change.

"You look at all your senior people. You decide whether you're going to retain them or make a change. When I look at my senior staff, I look for energy, and men and women with high aspirations. You don't get a second chance to make a selection. If you haven't done it right the first time, you're in trouble."

Bruce Heilman says that in all his years, he doesn't believe he was a close friend of anyone on his senior staff. He was friendly, of course. But that's an important distinction.

Eleanor Roosevelt said: "You can't expect to make friends of everyone. And you're not going to make everyone happy. That's true of even the small circle you work with. You had better recognize that early on and get on with your life and your work."

James Fisher has an interesting take on this. He feels that day to day intimacy destroys illusions. It should be avoided. Distance becomes more acceptable as it is understood.

"To my knowledge, there is no research that concludes that too much distance is a problem for people who want to be successful presidents."

He says that in his experience, some very effective presidents are considered overly remote and distant. But this condition almost invariably helps the leader who can then demonstrate unusual humanness by occasional forays into the open.

The lesson on all this is to know yourself. You are not going to be stand-offish all of a sudden for the sake of being remote. Neither should you become very close friends with any on your staff. That can lead to problems and be destructive. John Bailey says, "Friendly, but not friends."

There's something else. I believe every college should have on its staff a vice president in charge of constant renewal. That's it! Vice President, Constant Renewal. I also suggest a Vice President for WOW! (With the exclamation mark).

I'm stretching, of course. But you do want a senior staff with an ebullient spirit. Fervent for the future. Impatient to begin knowing that everything is possible if they believe it's possible. Thirsty to pursue new ideas. Wellsprings of audacious energy and activity. As Chesterton once observed, "Enthusiasts soon understand one another."

I have worked with college presidents who handle their senior staff with a whip and a chair. But you know better. You understand that a staff is dysfunctional when it feels it must obey you. When that happens, you are managing the staff— not leading.

You understand that you must accept the responsibility, and the blame, when necessary. You pass on the credit and praise. Indira Ghandi said her grandfather told her there are two kinds of people. "There are those who do the work and those who take the credit. Try to be in the first group. There is less competition there."

You take pride in your staff when work is completed successfully and objectives fulfilled. You take your greatest satisfaction when the staff says, "we did it ourselves."

At times, you get unexpected results. Count on it. Let me recount an old Chinese fable.

It is about a Mandarin who for years stood along the river fishing. But instead of a hook, he used a straight pin.

The word of this curious behavior spread throughout the land until it finally reached the Emperor— who came himself to see this strange fisherman. What could anyone hope to catch with such a hook?

"For what are you fishing?" asked the Emperor.

The answer was serene. "For you, my Emperor," the Mandarin said.

You will get unexpected results from your staff. I promise. You are beginning a journey of continuing exploration and reinvention. You have the ability to rally senior colleagues. You have an eye for talent and keen coaching skills, and you exude unbounded optimism.

You are a college president. You have caught the brass ring of life. All it took was a Ph.D. Passion. Hunger. And deep Desire.

9

DEEP WATER GREATNESS
(Your College Can Never Be Better Than Your Faculty)

You have heard about the college president who was hospitalized with a grave illness. He had to miss the faculty meeting where he was typically an attender.

At the end of the meeting, the group spoke about the president's illness and hospitalization. They took a vote to wish him a speedy recovery.

The vote was 68 to 54!

One of the presidents I visited with for this book referred to her faculty as, "a thousand points of no." I've heard it said that every organization has problems…but only a college has a faculty. Every president has moments when he isn't sure whether his faculty members are following him or chasing him.

But you know better. You understand full well that the faculty stands at the intersection of what your college is and what you hope it to be.

"I overheard two faculty members talking." This is James Johnson telling me about a conversation he happened to catch in the college's cafeteria during his second week on campus.

"Why would she ever want to come to Ohio Valley as a student. She was, after all, a merit scholar."

Johnson was incredulous. You can be certain he dealt with the situation.

"I can assure you that was the last time I heard that sort of a statement from one of our teachers." But the problem was, the faculty at Ohio Valley was lacking in spirit and passion for the college. There may have been exceptions, but not many.

"I knew one of my first tasks was to pump new life into the faculty. I had to motivate them to reach higher expectations. I had to keep raising the bar."

Should anything like this ever happen to you, just emulate the Jesuits and call it a teaching opportunity. If you are willing to accept mediocrity in your faculty, that's what you will get. A mediocre faculty.

Lisa Ryerson tells me it's essential that the faculty know who is in charge. It could have been a problem for her.

"I had been around so long, some of the faculty even remembered me as an undergraduate. Not all of the faculty were happy with the decision to select me. I knew that. I even knew those who were somewhat opposed.

"From our very first meeting in those early days, I wanted them to know I was in charge. I was the president. The faculty had to understand that.

"I never miss a faculty meeting. It would have to be something most unusual to have me miss. And I chair the meeting. In our situation, for our size college, I think that's important."

Your presence at faculty meetings, whether you chair it or not, and your involvement with the faculty are important. At times, it can be difficult. You may even reach out for an excuse not to attend— what Bob Dylan called, "shelter from the storm." But you stand up to it. You are the leader.

Jake Schrum says: "I made it a practice in my first weeks to meet with the entire faculty. Every member. I arranged for a luncheon or a meeting somewhere special where we could be together alone. There were a lot of lunches, but it was really worthwhile.

"They knew I listened to them. I really listened. I wanted to know what their hopes and dreams were— or whether they even had any hopes and dreams. In those early months, I got to know my faculty very well, the good and the not so good."

That was a refrain I heard in almost all of my visits. It was a common thread woven throughout the fabric on what is considered an inviolate truth.

"One of the problems I find that most presidents get into if they are set on a failure course is that they forget what it's all about." Here's how Jake Schrum puts it in focus. "It's all about the student. That takes a certain amount of humility for an ego-driven president to understand. But that's what it's about.

"You have to keep reminding the faculty that it's about the students. There are times, in all of the discussions that they seem to forget that. I like to keep reminding them of that on a pretty regular basis.

"Everything we do ought to be concentrated on helping students reach their highest aspirations. That's the ultimate task of the faculty."

Sue DeWine agrees entirely. She believes that no matter what the discussion is among faculty members, the focus must be on the students.

"When I arrived, I found a cranky faculty. They were very upset about the conditions that existed at the college. I made it clear to everyone I came in contact with that our focus had to be on the students. That seems so obvious but for some reason, I find it is not always the case. The faculty need to be reminded of that."

James Fisher knows of some presidents who had serious difficulty in the first month. "That happens when there's not enough consultation with the board and too much consultation with the faculty. The new president has to remember that she is in charge, not the faculty."

Fisher also worries about faculty members who have access to trustees. It's so easy to have that happen, but it usually means trouble. The chair of the board needs to make it quite clear to trustees that discussions about the college and the president are off-limits.

"Some of you know the faculty quite well, some of you had them for courses when you were undergraduates. Some see them socially. But when it comes to any sort of an issue about the president or the college, that needs to be something I handle." That's the sort of thing the chair needs to say to trustees.

"In my early days," Georgia Nugent tells me, "I tried to meet with as many faculty as I possibly could. I also offered to meet with every academic department. There are nearly 30. I felt that would be very important. Not everyone picked me up on that suggestion. But with those I met with, it was entirely worth it."

The faculty is at the very front line of your college. No matter what else you do, nothing is more important than a faculty that is passionate about the college and willing to do anything that's necessary to create a transformational environment for the students.

In some cases, it may be necessary for you to make a change in attitude and direction. They need to understand that in today's world, change is all you can count on.

I am told that Richard Feynman once handed his secretary an exam to be distributed to his doctoral students. Feynman is a Nobel Laureate and one of the greatest mathematicians of the 20th Century.

His secretary scanned the paper and objected. "But Professor Feynman, these are the same questions you used last year. Won't the students already know the answers?"

"It's all right," replied Feynman. "The questions are the same, but the answers are different."

Change is not always easy. There is only one way to get anyone to do anything— and that is by motivating the other person to want to do it. There is no other way. You are the leader. You need to inspire your faculty to greater heights.

It's not that simple. Helping the faculty to become dedicated and devoted to the highest quality possible, to the transformation of their students, and to making certain each man and woman reaches their highest potential and aspirations— that may require a change in attitude. Change doesn't automatically happen.

In Winnie-The-Pooh, AH Milne wrote: "Here is Edward Bear, coming downstairs now, bump, bump, bump, on the back of his head. It is, as far as he knows, the only way of coming down stairs, but sometimes he feels that there really is another way, if only he could stop bumping for a moment and think of it."

You are the leader. You are in charge of writing a new story for your faculty.

You understand heart and soul that the college's status (and recruiting and fundraising) is determined on the basis of whether you have a so-so faculty, a good faculty, or a great one.

You are success-driven. You want a great faculty. You won't settle for anything less.

You have little tolerance for institutional restraints. Your college's mission is to effectively serve its students. To wring from your students nothing less than their greatest talents and attributes. To help them reach the unmet yearnings within each individual's grasp.

Nothing else matters.

Unfortunately, in some situations it can be the other way around. You will work hard not to become a prisoner of iron-forged faculty habits, hoary practices, and outdated attitudes.

I spoke to James Edwards about Esther Barrazone's first few months at Chatham College. He was a trustee at the time.

He's a perfect person to have as a trustee. He is thoughtful, wise, speaks his mind, and is a roaring advocate for the college and Esther. (He is, also, president of a significant Pittsburgh foundation— and it doesn't hurt to have a major funder on the board!)

"It was a terrible situation," Edwards tells me. "The faculty ruled the roost at the college. It was a critical part of the major problem at Chatham.

"When Esther came to the college as president, she had to stare-down the faculty. She had to do it right away. This was something that had to be done for the future of the college.

"She was able to do it and she did it magnificently. We were swollen with too many faculty, too many tenured, and too many visiting faculty. Esther was able to make the necessary changes. She saved the college."

The Economist once described tenure as a promise to professors that, "They can think or idle in paid peace, accountable to nobody." That can be a burden the president might face in a new situation.

When I talked with Esther about the comment from Edwards, I asked her what the reaction was to the changes she had to make. She tells me that she had to let everyone know that change was coming. But it didn't happen without its problems.

"There came a time in my early weeks when I had to let one of our favorite faculty members go. When I came to the campus the next morning after the announcement, there were sheets hanging out the resident hall windows with nasty comments about me. It wasn't very pleasant."

But she says she worked very closely with the faculty before all the cuts. They understood how grievous the situation. They didn't like it but they knew it had to be done. (I call this the Broccoli Syndrome: You don't like it but you know it's good for you.) She was able to achieve all of the reductions successfully because she wasn't doing it on her own.

"Sure you make mistakes. I made tons of them. But you keep plunging ahead.

"The problem was that it was hard for us to get really good faculty because the college was on *financial watch*. The whole world seemed to know about it. I had to give the board and the faculty hope."

In some cases like this, like Esther, you may need an intravenous injection of courage. Just think about John Paul Jones and his declaration about needing the fastest ships, "For I intend to go in harm's way."

That's part of the secret. Hope. Confidence. Your vision. Your job is to be transformational.

I had a problem with a college in New England. The president had strong organizational credentials but no prior experience in higher education. He had a mean temper and a forbidding personality. A cross word from him scattered the sparrows from the trees.

For some reason he felt he had to take an adversarial position with the faculty. Soon, it was *him* against *us*. He somehow felt that if he acted as a wolf, he would beget a faculty of sheep.

He did not understand how a faculty bereft of purpose and

leadership affects the spirit and soul of the students. And how this, in turn, heightens attrition. Ultimately there is a ripple effect that somehow decreases the enrollment of the incoming freshman class.

The president was practicing what Nobel Laureate Richard P. Feynman called, "active and boundless irresponsibility." I was at one of the faculty meetings where he presided (ranted). I was on pins and needles. It was like watching an infant play with a valuable Steuben vase.

The faculty finally revolted. A committee was appointed to meet with the board chair.

"How serious is it?" asked the board chair.

There was a litany of offenses and affronts (at least he wasn't accused of making any Graven Images). They said his most flagrant problem is he doesn't know how to listen.

The president was gone the following year. The damage was done. But the faculty rallied. Out of every crisis comes the opportunity to be reborn. He had taken great pride in claiming he was a man of iron. It is good to remember that the same hammer that forges steel shatters glass.

You are the leader.

You are expected to deliver exceptional results during your tenure as president. It begins with the first 120 days. One of the most important aspects is your relationship with your faculty. You help them believe in the canon of the possible.

Evans Whitaker says, "I felt my first task as president was to keep hope alive. There had to be an infusion of hope and confidence.

"I spoke about this everywhere I went. With everyone I spoke with. At every faculty meeting. I kept hope alive. I let everyone know about my objectives for the near future and I affirmed the great values of the college.

"I felt my job was to motivate the faculty, inspire the staff, build confidence with the alumni, and diffuse any conflicts and issues there might be. I wanted to serve as a symbol of confidence and optimism."

Evans makes it quite clear to me that he succeeded a popular president who was successful in saving the college during his tenure. But this was a new day and a new president. There had to be a new vision.

The faculty makes the difference. And even though you may have a chief academic officer, it is the president who leads and inspires the faculty. In a sense, you are the chief cheerleader for the faculty.

The challenge is that often you are left teetering between the faculty on the one side and the board on the other. In a sense, you are caught between a dog and a lamppost.

You want a faculty that is highly ambitious for the college. They see no limit to its growth. They are excited about the future. That's what you hope for. But that's not always what happens. One college president told me that a committee meeting of her faculty is a *cul-de-sac* to which ideas are lured and then quietly strangled.

"The problem is," says James Fisher, "the tendency for many presidents is to want to spend too much time with the chief academic officer. That's an important relationship— but the new president must let that person do their job. In fact, I have seen situations where the new president, with a background as an academic officer, acts as if he was still the chief academic officer.

"I see a difficult future for that kind of person. Some college presidents fail because they are more comfortable in the faculty dining room than at the country club. One of the major roles of the new president is to raise funds. A president who still wants to be the chief academic officer is going to run into problems."

As the president, you are the faculty's chief booster, its roaring advocate. But you let your chief academic officer do her job (and be thankful because at times, that can become nasty).

I had a faculty member at Mississippi College tell me that she thought the president's job can be really difficult. She said the president is described as ambivalent and unable to make a decision if he won't make major cuts in someone else's department budget. But if he cuts my budget, I call him insensitive and thoughtless.

Faculty are disappointed when you as the president fail to be leading the parade on its behalf. You have to be their greatest champion.

You wish for your institution the brightest, most caring, most effective faculty possible. You know this will make the difference in being just a good college or a great college.

What you seek is what Saul Bellows calls, "deep water greatness." That kind of a faculty will give you an ability to navigate the institution by the brightest stars.

The focus of your faculty has to be on your students. Their job is to teach, guide, explain, help, and nurture the students. That's what it is all about. This is certainly the college's most noble objective.

Sometimes it takes more for the president than just having a good rapport with the faculty— and being persuasive and unre-lenting. Sometimes it's sheer luck— like getting safely across a busy New York street.

It's easy to develop your faculty to their highest productive level. You let them get involved.

But James Fisher points out that there is a very important distinction in the power you give them. The president (not the board) grants the faculty the *privilege* (italics for emphasis) of participating in decision making. It is important to note that this is the president's prerogative, not the board's.

You delegate. You increase their responsibility to appropriate levels. You encourage them to participate. You make them stand on tip-toes. Most of all, you help them reach their loftiest aspirations.

It often happens, perhaps it's inevitable, that faculty want to get in the good graces of the new president. That's only human nature.

It is easy to get trapped. You end up giving time to a faculty member who cannot really be of help. Some are incapable, outdated, or actually not part of the culture you hope to impose.

There will be a lot of faculty who want to get your attention and influence you. But everyone is watching. That's why you have to be particularly careful about how you handle the faculty in your early days.

In the case of Georgia Nugent, she sent an e-mail to every faculty member before she began her presidency. What a brilliant idea.

She announced she'd be coming to Kenyon and was looking

forward to greeting each of them in person. She asked them to tell her: What's the one thing you're particularly proud of regarding the college? She also asked, what would be the one thing you would change?

She received a huge response. She tells me it was immensely helpful. She, of course, responded to all of the e-mails.

John Hood says that he met with the Faculty Senate often during his early days. He called special meetings. There are about 200 in that group.

He says he was totally transparent with them about everything that had to be done. Did he agree about everything they told him or suggested? Obviously not, but they knew where he stood on all important matters.

Hood visited every department in the first 120 days. Every single department! After a thorough discussion, he told them he wanted to have them give him five take-aways. He did this at every visit. It was immensely helpful.

Mary Pat Seurkamp tells me the faculty plays a very special role at Notre Dame. She said that when she started, she knew she had to move fast. The culture needed to be changed. Being the first lay president in the history of the college, there were some obstacles and huge hurdles to overcome.

"In the first 120 days, I managed to meet with every major academic person. I didn't miss anyone. I asked them what they were going to do to help me move the college forward. I knew I couldn't do it without their endorsement and support."

Her selection to be president was not a popular one. The board was split. Not because of Mary Pat Seurkamp's credentials, but because she would be the first president not a member of the cloth.

In fact, it was so contentious that it ended up in a divided board. Several who were against her election resigned. "But I knew if I had the faculty with me, I was on the right track and would make it."

Scott Miller says that in the first few weeks, he met with all of the senior faculty. He feels that's essential.

"I wanted to hear how they felt and what they had to say. I wanted to know about their vision and aspirations. I knew what mine were but I wanted to hear from them. I listened.

"The faculty is so key to everything that happens. I want to make certain they don't feel ignored.

"When I met with them, I just let the agenda flow. I'm certain they felt there was no structure to the meeting— but indeed there was. I wanted to hear from them. And I listened. I feel, by the way, listening is an essential ingredient to being a good president, particularly in those early days."

Steven Jennings says in the first month or so, you talk with all the faculty. What you are trying to determine is the rhythm of the culture. He feels he needs to hear the music of their mind and understand the spirit of their heart. But it's important, he cautions, that you not listen to the wrong people.

B. Joseph White didn't waste any time when he became president of the University of Illinois.

"In my first days, I went to see all the key faculty. They are critical to your success.

"I would go to them instead of having them come to my office. I think that's a good strategy for a lot of reasons. For one thing, I get to see their surroundings and how they keep their office. But it also allows me to leave when I am ready to do so. You learn a great deal by visiting with them in their office."

Here's what I find. If you expect the very best from your faculty, and you let them know that— you are almost never disappointed. It's your job to keep raising the bar. If you are willing to settle for a so-so faculty unwilling to strive and of lowly ambition, that's almost always what you will get. A so-so faculty.

I liken that in some ways to the experiment that was done with fleas. (You will please forgive the comparison I make of a faculty and fleas.) Have you heard about this bit of research.

They put fleas in a cardboard box. Then they put a lid on the box. As the fleas jumped, they kept hitting their heads on the roof of the box.

Within a short space of time, every flea inside the box was jumping just below the level of the lid so they wouldn't hit their heads. Then the research people took the lid off the box.

Guess what happened?

The fleas continued to jump— but just below the level of where the lid had been. They were not going to risk hitting their heads again. Here's the important lesson— they were also not jumping to their highest possible capacity.

Your job is to inspire the faculty to reach their highest possible capacity and their most fervent professional promise.

You shouldn't be surprised if you find a faculty member sprinkled like itching powder over a host of irritants and objections. It happens. You are, after all, working with some very bright people. Articulate. Some with egos as large as the founder's statue on the quadrangle.

You will find that in your early weeks if you seem to hesitate or perhaps misstep, you'll get a lot of advice from the faculty. Be prepared. Mark Twain said: "Anyone who has a bull by the tail knows five or six things more than someone who hasn't." That could be you.

Somehow, you make a room for spirited, obstreperous, creative, inner-directed people. To have a truly vital and fertile faculty, you want them to be enemies of rote and status quo. Be ready for them to upset the applecart (even your applecart) by thinking of new and better ways of doing things.

Some colleges have a faculty with an unwritten law. It says, don't bother us. We won't change. We stand firm for stagnation.

There is the story of Woodrow Wilson when he was president of Princeton University. He was incredulous. "How can I democratize this university," he demanded, "if the faculty won't do everything I ask."

"One of us" is a phrase often used by the faculty to describe a new president in the first three months or so on the job. After that, it's "she's a nice person but doesn't seem to have a clear agenda or know anything about running the college."

Welcome the malcontent. You must encourage and support new ideas. A crank can be a troublemaker and an irritant. Just remember that a crank also ignites an engine. The seeds of faculty progress are often rooted in some discontent.

You perhaps have heard about the poor chap who had overslept. They began pounding on the bedroom door to wake him up.

"John, get up. Get up. John get up."

They kept pounding and finally opened the door and entered the bedroom.

"John, you've got to get up. You've overslept again. It's very late."

"I'm not going to school. I'm never going back again. None of the students talk to me. They all think I'm strange. Even the janitors think I'm terrible. And the teachers all hate me."

"John, you've got to get up and go. You're the president of the college."

It could happen to you. Just keep in mind that the most effective faculty should be in a perpetual evolution. (Note, I did not say revolution!) If they are standing still, engrossed and enamored by the venerated past, you're in deep trouble.

When I spoke with William Carl, III, he told me in the first few weeks, he spent three hours with every faculty member. You read that correctly: Three hours with every faculty member. He says it was worth it.

In every case, he told them about his four sacred (quite appropriate for a Theological Seminary) Ss.

No Secrets
No Surprises
No Subversion

Lots of Support

Then after his individual meetings, he talked about his Ss at the next few faculty meetings.

He felt his job was to exude optimism and confidence. He gave the faculty a heavy dose of high expectations and hope. It paid off. The same promising assurance and enthusiasm was also shared with the board and alumni.

When he became president of the seminary, there were a number of serious issues. (He prefers calling them opportunities.) The institution is now in its best condition, financially and in enrollment, in its history. He says the faculty deserves a major share of the credit for that.

Let the four Ss work for you. It's quite a clear understanding of what you should expect from the faculty. If you achieve that, the faculty will propel the institution forward in wondrous ways.

Harold Kolenbrander says that a college can have better buildings and facilities than they presently have. It's possible, also, that they could have a better administrative team that heads them. But, he says, colleges can never be better than the faculty who teach there.

That says it all.

10

A GREAT FUTURE FOR COMPLEXITY
(You Are The Change-Agent)

There's a *Peanuts* cartoon. Lucy is lecturing her younger brother Linus about all sorts of information that makes no sense at all to Linus. Charlie Brown is listening. He eventually comments that poor Linus is going to have to go to school twice as long as anyone else. First, he must learn all the nonsense Lucy has just taught him. Then he must unlearn everything he knew before.

Sometimes, it's like that.

In your early days at the college, you may have to *unlearn* a lot of the past— the culture of the college and the traditional way of doing things. Even if the college has been successful in the past, that is no assurance of future vitality and growth.

The spirit which welcomes change is a fragile thing. At times you take a lesson from Adlai Stevenson who said the most difficult problem for all of us— is not to learn more, but to unlearn the past.

There needn't be major changes that are necessary for every new president. Georgia Nugent said that when she went to Kenyon College, very few changes were needed, certainly nothing urgent.

You may not be as fortunate. One college president told me that when you first arrive, if everything seems to be going quite well, you have obviously overlooked something.

In many situations for the new president, changes that have to be made immediately, are grave and severe. At many colleges, you don't need a formula for thriving in this bewildering, changing world. You need a blueprint for just surviving. For the president, in these unconventional times, it requires uncommon wisdom and unimpeded decision-making.

"I'll tell you why we have been so successful," says Bill Gates. "We run like mad— and then we change directions."

Jim Fisher tells me that holding on to the past and maintaining the *status quo* is always wrong.

"One of the major functions of the new president is to institute change. If you stand still, you're losing.

"Change is important because if you're not moving forward, you're moving backward. In today's world, you can't stand still. There's no such thing as that. Change is essential on every campus. That's one of the important things the new president has to undertake in the first few months."

Joseph White agrees. "To be a successful president, you have to achieve change— important consequential change. It has to be done quickly." Making change successfully is one of the new president's greatest and most important challenges. In many situations, that's why you've been brought to the college.

There are extraordinary changes taking place in higher education. It is a phenomenon that is fueled by massive forces. Some of these you can exert some control over. There is new technology, new markets, and high school seniors with new attitudes. Your job is to anticipate and act.

The opportunities were never greater. But in order for your college to thrive, you need to determine the changes that are necessary on your campus— the ineffable, sometimes irrational, and often unexplainable.

Indeed, in order to flourish, you had better take a very careful look at your situation in your first few days. Your college exists in a world where everything must happen better, faster, and at less cost.

Those young men and women who consider your college for entrance are smarter, more selective, and more demanding. They have higher expectations and academic quality, more extra activities, and better overall performance. And *sacre bleu*— they want it at a lower cost.

We have gone from an era when the big fish eat the small. Now it's the fast eat the slow.

You, as a new president, are in the business of change management. Your job is to enhance and improve the present while creating an exciting future.

You don't have the luxury of time. Your situation may call for a serious disruption of the fabric of the past. You eschew crusty rigidity and stubborn complacency.

Many new presidents put more energy and resources into preserving what they have— rather than putting their priority into that which they don't have. A successful president does not let present pressures win over future opportunity.

When you make decisions for change, you may not win any popularity contests. There are those who wish to hold on to what they believe is the golden past.

There will be the naysayers and handwringers. When they hear about the changes you are planning, you must spend your days being like Odysseus— tied to the mast and not listening to the sirens.

You need to have a creative discontent. You have to learn to step outside the comfort zone. You must enhance and improve the present while creating an exciting future.

In today's world, you must leave behind old solutions. It's not always easy. John Cage said, "I can't understand why people are frightened of new ideas. I'm frightened of the old ones."

It's not easy. One day, very early in your tenure, you turn a corner in your mind, do a back somersault, jiggle the kaleidoscope, and I don't know what else. Then suddenly you're ready for the plunge.

Esther Barazzone speaks first-hand about what it's like.

"When the board hired me, they made it clear they wanted change and they told me they were willing to dare to make it happen.

"They felt in the past they had given too much control to the president and were asleep at the switch. They didn't want that to happen again. But they didn't want to interfere with the changes I wanted to make and they certainly understood the boundaries of a good trustee.

"They wanted to make certain they were watching things carefully— but what they were most insistent on was change. They weren't certain what that should be. But they knew things had to change.

"In the first 120 days, I got very busy making changes. The board wanted innovation. I went to work on that. I also had to let some of the faculty go. It simply had to be done.

"What I did in those early days really helped turn the college around. Now we are on a straight projectory that has been going up every year since I got here. In the past five years we've grown 75 percent in enrollment and in fundraising, all due to the changes I made in those early months."

When Mary Jane England became president of Regis College, it was days away from bankruptcy and total collapse.

"I didn't have the luxury of time. Decisions for changes had to be made immediately. The school was in a crisis. In the first weeks, I had to let some of the senior staff go who were not pulling their weight. There wasn't time to try to coax and coach them along. I had to cut expenses dramatically.

"It was a traumatic time. Some of the changes were very difficult. But I wouldn't take any of those early decisions back. We are now on the right track. Those early changes were the thing to do."

John Hood tells me that one of the major questions you must

ask yourself in the early weeks is to determine what you would do differently. How will it be possible to make the changes that are necessary?

"You don't always make the right decisions. What is important is that you make the best decisions you possibly can at the time. Changes are essential. You use the best lens you have.

"When you have all the information you can possibly gather and all the discussions with key individuals involved, then it's up to you. It can be lonely. You've got to decide what you are going to do. You don't do your university any good by deferring the decisions."

At times, it will be tough. Count on it.

You may remember Colonel Nicholson, the perfectionist who builds an extraordinary bridge. There comes a time, however, when he has to blow it up. He utters the famous lines, "Oh my God, what have I done."

What do you do when you have pivotal and perilous decisions. Some require bold (perhaps frightening) action. You may feel stuck. It's keeping you up at night. Here are some good questions to ask.

1) Do you have enough information? 2) Is there someone else I haven't spoken with yet whose input might help move this forward for me (perhaps your mentor)? 3) Is it quite clear that I am the one to make this decision?

Be certain to ask yourself if 4) Can I come at this from a different perspective. 5) By any chance, am I afraid to make a decision (be honest)? 6) Am I over-dissecting the issue (analysis paralysis) in order, perhaps, to avoid that moment when a decision has to be made— what Robert Frost calls, "Your passage to your journey's end."

Take courage in what Esther Barazzone tells me.

"I let everyone know that change was coming. In those first 120 days you are committed to making changes. You have to work at it quickly and decisively. Learning, learning, learning about the situation.

"At times, you can't even catch your breath. Getting a handle on things is what you work as quickly as possible. The important thing is that you make the decision. You don't delay. Get on with it. You'll get it right."

Not every new president faces a desperate situation— a campus on the brink of despair, discouragement, and dismay. Some are more fortunate.

Take Richard Jewell for instance. He was on the board for 25 years— then was elected president.

Dick had the advantage of knowing the college very well. He knew the senior staff and faculty. The academics of the college were effectively in place.

There was one very important necessary change. He felt his most urgent job in the first few months was "to open the college up." He wanted to immediately raise the level of involvement and ownership by the board and the faculty.

"I wanted to make certain in those first early months that no one said, 'It's always been done this way before.' But truly, the college was doing so very well, and there weren't a great number of changes that had to be made. I was very fortunate in this regard. I just had to add some ingredients to the ongoing mixture."

I mentioned Georgia Nugent earlier in this chapter. Her early days were happy ones. When she arrived, she says she was very fortunate.

"There was nothing broken, there were no secrets, no hidden agendas. Actually, it was a love affair from the very start. Actually, the next three years were a honeymoon."

Even when things are going exceedingly well, you need to be vigilant. Let's say that enrollment has increased dramatically, you are being much more selective about the students you enroll, a greater percentage than ever are paying full tuition (praise be to the gods), fundraising has hit an all time high, and there is wonderful esprit among the faculty. Students notice you are strolling around the campus humming Beethoven's *Ode to Joy*.

But be wary. Just when you think all is going extremely well and show signs of settling into a groove, the needle jumps and skitters to another track.

Let me tell you about the *Sigmoid Curve*. For colleges that are doing exceedingly well, this is a particularly significant concept.

I'll describe it and then have a drawing of the S-shaped phenomenon which will help you visualize it.

It demonstrates the diminishing returns and the evolution of activities— even in a flourishing college. Stay with me on this.

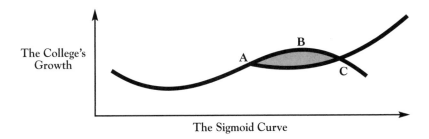

The Sigmoid Curve

Things begin to *max out* (**A** on the drawing) after a period of growth. It happens to corporations, a product's life-cycle, and even with love and some relationships— the rise and fall. It happens at many successful colleges.

Luckily, there is life beyond the curve. The secret of constant growth for the college is to start a new *Sigmoid Curve* before the first one begins a downward slide. This is what it looks like.

I've designated **A**, as the time where you begin anticipating a possible drop-off in the activity. You are growing, but you notice there is a bit of waxing and waning. There is still momentum, but not quite what it was before.

It is at this stage that a different plan needs to be put into effect. Usually quite promptly. That should be done before you reach **B**. **A** represents the most important time to step back, contemplate the college's progress on the curve, and consider launching a new effort.

By point **B**, the slide has already begun. At point **C**, it is too late for the college.

Your job is to begin taking action at **A**. You must not wait until you reach **B**. The trouble often is that when you finally figure out where *it* is at . . . somebody moves *it*.

Annie Dillard writes that, "The thing we desperately need is to face the way it is." Being in the leadership role means you have to face the truth with the bark stripped off.

The president has to make decisions regarding change, quite often without an opportunity for careful study. You require immediate action.

There are even times when your solutions are the seeds of new problems. But there's good news. As Donald M. Michael points out,* most of the time situations don't get entirely out of hand when changes are made. That should give you some comfort.

You may think you understand the situation in those early days. But what you don't understand is that the situation has just changed. That's how fast things move. In seeking answers, you cannot draw uncritically from the past. But neither can you reject it. Your job is to disdain and abandon what is unworthy.

You cast aside the old that didn't work. You build on the truths that are still vital to your mission and your college's essential tradition. But you look to the future. You face the present challenges, though some may be quite uncomfortable.

You keep in mind that your profound responsibility as the new president is to focus on the future. You speak in the future tense.

You maintain a disquieting distaste for the rusted shackles of the past. You are vigilantly open and aggressively attuned to change. You push your work to the very edge where myth and the past meet spirit and growth. You give a high definition to what is relevant and essential to the college.

I was at a Faculty Senate meeting. The provost announced in jest that colleges and universities are places where the First Law is: "Nothing should be done for the first time." (I thought it was quite humorous but there wasn't a smile in the group.)

The world is moving so fast these days that the president who says it can't be done by her college is generally passed by a college that is doing it. The problem is that the person who stakes her presidency on change is too often on her own.

*Competence and Compassion In An Age of Uncertainty

Take some comfort in what Saint John wrote centuries ago on the lonely, obscure island of Patmos: "Behold, you must make all things new. Former things are passed away."

Some colleges have hardening of the categories. You must be unwilling to tolerate something that is so-so. The real problem is when something is not so bad you are willing to dump it, but not good enough that you are willing to keep it. Well, if you're willing to put up with that, you'll never be able to change something for the better and you will not have a successful tenure.

It's not always simple or clear-cut. Every president who is willing to take risks understands that the best solution is not often the obvious one. At times it's hard to know the difference between a red light and a green one.

In many situations, the new president faces changes that must be made. In other colleges, what is needed is a total transformation. For some, a step forward is required. For others, it's a quantum leap that's necessary. It may require eccentric experimentation and a radical departure of rule.

Your past experience may not be a helpful guide. What other colleges have done will not be a solution either. It's not a case of monkey-see, monkey-do.

The successful president will not resist change. She will seek it. There must be a capacity for courage, and a passion to learn and to grow. The focus is on change. You can count on it at your college.

The only thing constant in change is change itself. It's nothing new. When Adam and Eve left Eden, it's quite possible that

Adam may have said: "We're now entering into a period of transition."

"I predict a great future for complexity and change," said E.B. White. Never expect a stable or comfortable future. Change is the constant.

I've heard it said of some presidents that they do not lead the parade but find out where it is going, and try to get ahead of it. You are different. You understand you are at your most effective best when you are resolute and quite clear about what you want. The next important step is to determine how to get there.

The presidents who have blazed new paths for their college have always been precedent-breakers. It is often a president who believes in her own ideas. Who can think and act without a crowd to back her. Who is not afraid to stand alone. She understands Emerson's admonition: Always, always, always do what you are afraid to do.

She is bold, original and resourceful. She has the courage to go where others have never been and to do what others have never done. These are the presidents who leave their mark on the college.

New ideas can make life at times intolerable for the new president. There are so many on the campus who have an emotional tie to the past. There can be the temptation to play it safe.

But if you stop innovating, pursuing new directions, and making necessary changes, you and the college will be standing still. You may not notice it at first. It happens slowly, like paint flaking away. Or worse, you may be on a downward slide. You will be much like Mike Campbell describes going broke in *The Sun Also*

Rises: "Gradually and then suddenly."

For the new president, leading the charge can be a heavy and turbulent burden. At the same time, it is exhilarating and life-giving. But this is why you were chosen. Why you came. This is what it is all about. The great adventure.

For some on your campus, breaking tradition, and dealing with those who tell you, "we've never done this before"— what you are doing can seem like a dropped vase, cracked in all directions. Touch it and it will shatter.

Even younger colleges can be steeped in customs and practices that cause a stranglehold on progress. An older college may require an even closer examination of its grizzled traditions and its old way of doing things. The future is moving so fast that you're going to have to take your cue from Indiana Jones. When he was asked about his plan, his answer was: "I don't know. I'm making this up as I go."

There's plenty of room at the bottom. You understand fully that if you continue doing what you always did— you will always get what you always got. Your credo is *citius, altius, fortius*— faster, higher, stronger.

To assist the president, every college should have someone in charge of change and constant renewal. That would help you eschew what I call the *Barnacle Syndrome*.

The barnacle is confronted with the life-time decision about where it is going to live. Once it decides that, it spends the rest of its life with its head permanently cemented to a rock. Not moving, not thinking, not productive, and not changing.

Some college presidents are like the barnacle. Not the successful ones. Not you.

11

PUSH AND PULL
(You Are The Leader)

Which is it? An art? Or a science?

Leadership is both an art and a science— intersecting in wondrous ways. As Flaubert wrote, "I don't know what either is without the other." It propels your vision and commitment into action. Your leadership, as the new president, is the spark that ignites the fire.

Leadership is hard to define. It's like beauty. You know it when you see it. The French painter, Georges Braque, said: "The only thing that matters in art can't really be explained."

The president is the leader of the college. If there aren't leadership skills, the college falters. The president needs to be a high-achieving person. You have to love challenges and have rarely seen a hill you don't want to climb.

Joseph White has a great deal to say about leadership. In fact, he wrote a book on leadership you should read.* When he speaks,

---

*The Nature of Leadership: Reptiles, mammals, and the Challenge of Becoming A Great Leader (A fetching title! You'll understand when you read the book.)

you listen.

"Keep in mind, there is a great difference between leadership and management. It's not at all the same. You can be a good manager, but not a leader.

"Some presidents are good managers, but chances are they will not provide transformational growth in their college. Management is pretty much about order and control. Leadership is fundamentally about making change and achieving challenging goals."

The practice of leadership is not the same as the exercise of power. Jim Collins in his, *Good to Great,* points out that if a loaded gun is put to a person's head, you can get things done that might not be achieved otherwise. But that's not practicing leadership.

True leadership only exists if people follow when they have the freedom not to. If they follow because they have no choice, then you are not leading.

Joseph White makes it sound easy. When I asked him what it takes to be a successful president, he said you just simply need to keep in mind three things. First of all, you set high aspirations for the university and all of your staff. Second, recruit great people. Third, you bring tremendous energy and enthusiasm to work every day.

"I feel my job is to make individual dreams come true. That's in exchange for the staff and faculty helping make the dreams of the university come true."

White is emphatic about what he believes about a leader's attributes.

"For the president, energy is essential. Everyone feels it. It's contagious. If you have energy, it shows. If you don't have energy on a particular day, you make yourself be energetic. You force yourself. There are some days I simply have to wind myself up."

William James said, "The people who do really great things in this world are those who drive past the first layer of fatigue."

Some colleges are under-led and over-managed. Take a look at the typical Organization Chart for a college. There are some presidents who believe the chart has given them a body of followers. It has not. They have been given a staff who report to the president.

Whether the staff become followers depends on whether the president acts like a leader. Albert Schweitzer said: "Providing a proper example is not the main thing in influencing others. It is the only thing."

All presidents have vice presidents and deans who report to him. But that does not make the president a leader with followers. You are given a staff. You have to earn your followers. True leadership exists when people follow even though they have the freedom not to.

Here's the key. Managing is the science of getting other people to do things that need to be done. Leadership is the art of inspiring them to do that.

Managing is when **A** gets **B** to do something. Leadership is when **A** gets **B** to do what **B** might not normally have done but is inspired to do so by **A**. The true leadership of a president emerges from caring deeply about the college's goals and about the people you're leading toward those goals.

John Hood feels his major responsibility is helping his

staff, the faculty, and all around him to achieve their highest aspirations. He says you do this by sharing information, sharing power, and giving people an opportunity to express their initiative.

"You share responsibility. You build confidence in your people. You remove any barriers that may inhibit individual initiative and talent. You give people the resources they need. You resolve any conflicts that may exist that interfere with individual and group involvement and action."

The difference between a manager and a leader is significant in determining the success of the new president. It's a case of *push and pull*. The manager pushes his people to achieve objectives. The leader pulls his people up and forward by inspiring and motivating them.

Diana Chapman Walsh is the retired president of Wellesley College. She makes a case for there being a distinct difference between "transactional" and "transforming" leadership. It makes a great deal of sense.

Transactional is the win-win process when the president provides the staff with something they want in exchange for something he wants. That's the sort of thing that happens when there is a bonus for good work, recruiting more students, or raising more money.

She points out that this is management more than it is leadership. The "transforming leader-president" sees an existing need of a potential follower and develops a relationship that converts followers into believers. The "transforming leader-president" raises the level of drive and commitment of the followers.

In abbreviated form, I've indicated the characteristics of a manager and the attributes of a leader. It's easy for you to make the comparison.

I was surprised by the number of my presidents who spoke about the need for extraordinary levels of energy. Then, as I gathered more and more information about how they spent the first 120 days of their presidency, I began to understand. All were giving 10 and 12 hours a day to the job, and for most that also included weekends.

James Johnson walked into a situation that was in total disarray. He still works a heavy schedule but listen to what he told me about those early days.

"I worked seven days a week, every week during the first 3 months. I still maintain a heavy schedule. But in the first several months, I got into the office at 6:30 in the morning and never went to bed before 2:00 am. That was every single day."

Manager	Leader
• Manages what is in place at the college	• Innovates and is original
• Keeps the present alive	• Focuses on the future of the college
• System-oriented	• Develops people
• Controls	• Demonstrates trust and confidence
• Blames others	• Accepts blame for mistakes
• Efficient	• Effective
• Short range view	• Has long range perspective
• Dominates	• Empowers
• Asks how and when	• Asks why
• Concentrates on the bottom line	• Eye on the future
• Perpetuates the past of the college	• Challenges *status quo*
• Talks a lot	• Listens a lot
• Does things right	• Does the right things

The long days are a part of the job, and that requires a lot of energy. Georgia Nugent gets up early and exercises. She does a lot of reading in the morning and gets a lot of work done at home. She usually doesn't get to the office until around 10:00 am. She works until 6:00 pm and then she takes plenty of work home and right after dinner works until around 10:00 pm at the house.

"The problem is that once you are in the office, all of your time is pretty much transactional. You really don't have time to think and plan. You need to find other times to do that."

Jake Schrum tells me about one of the things that made the greatest impression on him. It was when Jake asked a very effective, well known college president what he felt was the most important factor to his success.

"He said it was having zest. I like that word. I think that must be a combination of energy plus passion. That's a pretty good formula for a college president.

"You need sound experience, of course, but that may not be the most important attribute. Some have intuitive feelings about how to get the job done. That's important. But what it really takes is zest— energy plus passion."

I found this to be true of all the successful presidents I visited with. There are extraordinary levels of energy. This is a characteristic inherent in some, but I'm convinced it can be enhanced with proper diet and exercise.

In this regard, and in most other important traits and personal gifts, you become what you want to be. It's important to know who you are. Just be a more intense version.

Here's the lesson: *You become what you want to be.*

Abraham Maslow wrote that people can be anything they want to be, but they must want it. "This is the urge we have called self-actualization . . . man's desire for fulfillment to become everything one is capable of becoming."

Being a leader is tough, arduous work. It requires constant energy. But this energy is not only driven and exhibited by the leader, it is multiplied and reinvested by staff, board members, and faculty who become infected with the fuel.

Sue DeWine tells me that she felt her job during the first three months was to touch as many people as possible.

"I met every single person I possibly could on the campus. I worked until seven or eight at night, and attended activities four nights every week. Every week. I hosted a lot of dinners. In the past year, we have had 2,000 people at the President's Home and in those first three months or so, I suspect I gave about 50 speeches."

"I think appearance and presence are terribly important." That's what Bruce Heilman tells me. He doesn't mean pretty or attractive. He refers mostly to a person who has immense energy. "That's what throws off the sparks, the excitement, the electricity."

"A president who exudes energy becomes a beacon light. I liken energy to passion. If you have that, it transforms others to the cause of the university."

Leaders are made, not born. *Fortune Magazine* ran this headline on a feature story: "Leadership Cannot Be Taught— But It Can Be Learned." It's a case of when the student is ready, the teacher will come.

You are in charge of your own performance. You can do it. Your greatness is not in being able to remake the college community, but in being able to remake yourself.

The successful college president consistently demonstrates an incredible energy, and endless stream of boundless vigor. It's what Joe White calls "the sparkle factor." Where does it come from, all this energy.

I'm convinced the energy is born out of a strong personal commitment. This is what drives the successful president forward and what motivates excitement in others. These energized presidents, they breathe life into the college and incite others to action. The only thing that can stop you . . .is you.

I heard this often on my visits, the importance of the inquisitive mind. Probing. Examining. Asking questions. Listening. These are characteristics of a leader.

As president, you never lose your sense of wonder. You are driven by curiosity.

I find curiosity is a prime attribute of the successful leader-president. The more they know, the more they seem to want to know. They are always probing, searching, exploring. They understand that the greatest lesson of all— is that they always have more to learn.

Coupled with this curiosity, the leader has a well-honed memory. This supports the information gathered by their curiosity. There is this insatiable will and desire to maintain a reservoir of facts and data. Leaders all seem to have these two qualities— curiosity and a finely tuned memory.

There are hundreds of superb books on leadership. Why have I devoted a chapter on the subject instead of directing you to one of these books. I already told you and I will mention it again.

In the first 120 days, everyone is scrutinizing. Everyone. Watching. Waiting. Deciding. The board, the staff, the faculty, the students, parents, and alumni— everyone.

One of the attributes the college universe will notice first of all is the new president's level of leadership. It's very likely more perception than reality.

But in those first 120 days, perception is everything.

In everything you do, in every act, in your journeys, in your speeches, and even on those weekends when you think no one is watching— everyone is! The leadership skills you exhibit in the first 120 days will lay the foundation for your long and successful tenure at the college.

You demonstrate your leadership in everything you do. You set the example. The British Essayist Matthew Arnold said, "Example is not a little thing."

John Gardner wrote what is very likely the single most outstanding book on leadership.* He should know. He was perhaps our country's most important statesmen of the last half of the 20th century.

Gardner defines leadership as: "The process of persuasion and example by which the college president induces others to take action. The direction of that action is in accord with the president's purposes."

You have heard the old saw: You can lead a horse to water but you can't make it drink. Your job as the leader is not to lead the horse to water. Nor is it to make it drink. Your job as the leader is

*On Leadership: John W. Gardner: 1990.

to make the horse thirsty.

I might add my own leadership postulate to that: You can lead a horse to water but if you can get him to float on his back— then you really have got something.

As a person advances in his career, from academic to president, from advancement to president, or whatever— I am convinced that behavioral changes are often the only significant ones that you can make. It's up to you to achieve what the ancient Greeks called *Arte*— to be the best you can possibly be.

Jack Welch is probably considered the most outstanding CEO in the last three decades. He has a Ph.D. in chemical engineering. But I have a feeling that none of the problems he encountered nor the decisions he made as CEO at General Electric were in any way related to his skill at chemical analysis or formulating plastics. The extraordinary talent he brought to his position was entirely behavioral.

Like Jack Welch, you have it in your power to be the leader you choose to be.

I want to remind you that Martin Luther King did not declare: I have a wonderful Long Range Strategic Plan. The basic ingredient of a successful president is to provide inspired and riveting vision. A dream for the future.

There are times in many situations your most important contribution is to give hope. I heard this time and time again.

Those around you need to be inspired with your dreams. You need to be perceived as a tuning fork ready to vibrate when properly struck. As the psalmist says, "Giving voice as crashing symbols." The purpose of leadership is to give hope.

The situation at Stephens College was tenuous. There had been declining enrollment over the past 20 years. The outside auditors were reassessing the financial situation. The news was quite grim. Desperate in fact.

Trustees thought they could borrow money to balance the budget. But they found they could not. Banks were betting against the viability of the college.

Wendy Libby felt that her job was to tell everyone the truth. The unvarnished truth. She was utterly clear and candid about letting everyone know what the actual situation was.

But here's the point. Everyone— the board, the faculty, the students— wanted hope. "I told them about my dreams for the future and I gave them hope."

Scott Miller tells me, also, about the importance of giving lofty anticipation and promise for the future.

"When I told the board I needed a $50 million commitment from them. I got it. It wasn't easy. But I got the commitment because I gave them hope."

There it is again— that essential ingredient of leadership: Giving Hope. Let me tell you what James Johnson says.

"My most important job in the first 120 days was to provide stability and hope to the university. I met with the faculty. I felt that my major job was to give them hope. I met with every department. I felt I had to let them know we were going to make it. I let them know that it may take a long time but that we were going to make it. I gave them my commitment and I gave them hope."

Jake Schrum tells me that he didn't spend a lot of time explaining to people what the college wasn't.

"I wanted to define what the college was. I wanted to determine and articulate what we do well. I wanted to give everyone hope.

"I told the board in my first 120 days that I needed cash, and that they would have to raise some money to give me some wiggle room. I gave them hope but I told them I needed funding very quickly. They came through in fine form.

"Some of the trustees were down in the dumps. I indicated I would be able to balance the budget in three years. Then I showed them how I was going to do that. It was hope plus my dedication to getting the job done. As a matter of fact, I was able to balance it in two years."

Sue DeWine tells me that even in her first few weeks, she met with over 400 people to talk about her dreams for the college. She laid out her goals. She gave them hope for the future.

The recent history of Chatham College is a horror story. It was in desperate shape. They knew they had to do something dramatic and they wanted an entrepreneurial president.

"I spent my time in those early three months," says Esther Barrazone, "explaining and speaking. Some people were horrified with our situation, but they appreciated getting a straight story.

"Most of all, I gave them hope that we could solve our problems. Because I was so candid in telling them about our situation, they believed it when I told them it can be turned around."

Since Esther's coming, the college is now in superb financial condition, enrollment continues to increase— one year more than the previous one, and fundraising is at an all-time high.

Evans Whitaker talks about the very difficult times at Anderson College. When he arrived, his mantra was: "We have to have hope." It paid off. They have had the best financial situation and the largest number of students in their history.

"Here's what I did," says Whitaker. "I initiated a program called, Future Search. Through a series of group meetings, small and large, we undertook a search for the future. We spoke only about our dreams and our hopes. All of this was done in my early weeks.

"Everyone knew we had a solid college. And an excellent past. I simply needed to give them hope for the future."

Leadership revolves around vision, ideas, direction, and dreams. It has most to do with your ability to inspire. You cannot possibly lead the college unless you motivate and leverage the beliefs of those around you. You give them hope.

You inspire others to dream more, do more, and become more. John W. Gardner says that leaders (read that: presidents) teach and they sell. They give hope. These may be too mundane to describe the lofty task of leadership, but as Gardner explains: "If leaders aren't teaching and selling and giving hope— they're not leading."

The successful college president must have integrity. That's where it begins. She must have vision. There must be the ability to rally and excite senior colleagues and faculty. There's more.

One thing that becomes clearer and clearer as I conduct my interviews is that integrity is spoken about as being one of the most important characteristics of a leader. That's where you gain the trust of others. As a new college president, you are called on to demonstrate that again and again.

Being an effective president is to know what path to take next. Leadership is taking it. Integrity is the enabling force that provides the leadership quality.

There must be coaching skills, an eye for talent, and the ability to recognize the correct choices. And to make decisions without postponement.

Your optimism is what brings out the best in others. It is contagious.

In the Appendix, I provide my list of the 101 characteristics of a leader. You mustn't be overwhelmed by this long roster. What is most interesting to me is that among the presidents I interviewed, all refer to integrity as being the *sine qua non* characteristic of being a great leader.

I have conducted a number of focus groups in colleges. I meet with staff leadership and select faculty. I ask what do you look for and what do you admire most in your president.

The response was fascinating— but may not surprise you. They told me: credibility, honesty, forward-looking, inspiring, and competent. In that order.

Please note: Academic acumen, effective in raising funds, and balancing the budget were not listed among the highest criteria.

You can be assured it doesn't take a charismatic personality, a showman, cheerleader, or circus stuntman. You don't have to do figure eights of presidential exactitude.

Credibility is the first law of leadership. And that means integrity. If you don't believe the messenger, you won't believe the message.

Credibility, has its roots from the Latin word *credo*. The meaning of *credo* is— I believe. High standards, personal values, impeccable integrity not only count. They are the only things that count.

There are other qualifications of a leader, of course. The president must have vision and be forward thinking. She defines and divines the future. She must give hope. All of these are important and she must be able to articulate these in such a way to inspire others to join her in this great college adventure.

David McCullough writes mostly about presidents and leadership. He was asked about some of the attributes he found most often in great leaders. He provides a list of seven. But he tells us what he feels is the most important.

"In the last analysis, character counts above all. It provides the foundation for everything else."

The difficulties and challenges that beset your path as a new president are incalculable. To find a way through the presidential maze and discover a path to excellence, stick to your own True North— your own core principles and values.

The successful college president honors the past, but at the same time, provides an easy fire escape. It is to the future where he seeks the college's greatest achievements.

True leaders don't manage things, they empower people. There is action. There is no time to wait. The successful new president does not react. He is proactive. Turning philosophy and creative intentions into bold action is what will determine the success of the new president.

You are less concerned with saying what you will deliver. There is far greater importance with delivering what you say you will.

If you want to have a great college, the president follows the *golden rule of leadership:* Just Do What You Say You Will Do. I have three necessary maxims to guide you: Know who you are, Say who you are, and then Do what you say. It's that simple.

In George Elliott's *Adam Bede*, Mrs. Poyser's stern advice is that, "You must be born again and born different."

Jim Collins, finds that leaders do not necessarily have towering personalities. Indeed, when charisma was being passed around, they seemed to have respectfully declined. (*Charisma*, by the way, comes from two Greek words meaning— Christ-like.) What Collins found interesting in the great leaders he studied was their humility.

Collins feels that is true because the president is ambitious first and foremost for the college and its dreams and vision for the future— not himself. They combine this obsessive ambition for the college with a ferocious dedication to do whatever it takes to make good on that ambition. Whatever it takes!

Humility. It's not about you. Jake Schrum is clear on the subject.

"One of the major issues that can cause the downfall of a president is arrogance. It's not about the president. You are the leader, but it's not about you. You are the vehicle for making it happen.

"You must never forget that students are your major focus. You want them to have a transformational experience. That's what it's all about. You happen to be in the right place at the right time."

There are three important qualities the new president should be endowed with. Humility. Humanity. Humor.

The successful college president breaks down old walls and creates new ideas and services. No neat little boxes and rigid organizational charts. The president is the first to break out of the boxes and inspire others to join— to open up their minds and tap their power and talent.

Thoreau wrote: "If you have built castles in the air, your work need not be for lost; that is where they should be. Now put the foundations under them."

You are the leader. It is your dreams, your vision, your castles in the air— you have been the inspiration. You know you are a successful leader when a person says, *I believe*. That is what Virginia Woolf called, "moments of being."

12

THOSE
PRECIOUS DAYS
(Three Important Lessons)

You Hear. But Do You Listen.

"I know you believe you understand what you think I said, but I am not sure you realize what you heard is not what I meant." That was Alan Greenspan speaking, former Chairman of the Federal Reserve Board. He went on to say, "If I seem unduly clear to you, you must have misunderstood what I said."

Let me set up a situation. Perhaps you can identify with it.

You are meeting with the Provost. She came into the office, unscheduled, and you have eleven important calls you have to return. Two are very urgent. You also have a meeting with the chair of the board you have to prepare for. The Provost is going on and on about a faculty member who missed two morning classes. Or was it something about the dress code?

You are hearing the Provost, you are supposedly communicating with her, you are making good eye contact, even nodding your head appropriately.

You hear, but you haven't been listening. Does this sound at all like you on some occasions.

Shame on you. You have tuned-out the Provost— you closed your earlids.

In the song, *The Sounds of Silence*, Paul Simon wrote:

> And in the naked light I saw
> Ten thousand people, maybe more—
> People talking without speaking.
> People hearing without listening.

Hearing and listening are two different functions, not to be misunderstood.

Hearing is physiological. Sound waves are received by the ear and transmitted to the brain. You have the ability to hear, some people better than others. But hearing is only the first step in the listening process. Listening is an immensely different behavior.

You won't find a clear definition of listening, but I'll give you one as good as any you will discover. *Listening is the process of receiving (that's hearing), interpreting, evaluating, and responding to messages.*

You already knew all of that.

I was surprised during my visits when presidents told me how much of their time in the first 120 days they spent in listening. Very likely, if measured, 80 percent of the new president's time was taken in listening.

Sue DeWine says that during the first month she met with as many people as she possible could. She had her regular and systematic routine for meeting with senior faculty. She met with students every possible moment she had.

"I spent a great deal of my time finding out everything I could. About the faculty, the students, and the college. I spent all of my days listening. Listening. Just listening."

Joseph White agrees. He encouraged everyone's participation and information in the early months.

"I find that listening is one of the most important aspects of my job. It certainly was during my first few months. A president has to be an excellent listener. Especially in those early days, you tend to listen to everyone. You begin sifting and sorting, but everyone's input counts."

You perhaps haven't given it much thought. You may not think of listening as being that important. It is. The central statement of faith in Judaism, by the way, begins with the word *Listen*.

You listen to gain new information and insights. If you don't listen actively, you're not getting all the information you need. That means channeling your entire attention on the subject at hand.

Of all the skills of leadership, listening is one of the most valuable. Yet it is one of the least practiced and prized. Some presidents listen only at times. They remain the ordinary leaders.

The effective presidents listen. They listen. And they listen. They are ever alert, constantly listening. In their office, at an event, meeting with a board member, and wherever. That's how they learn in advance of any unseen problems and unmet opportunities

Wendy Libby says, "In the first 30 days it is essential that everyone knows who you are and what you stand for. It's equally important that you listen. You listen carefully. You make people know you are listening."

Jake Schrum tells me that a serious problem of some of the failed presidents he knows is that they didn't listen. They may have heard, but they didn't listen.

"One of the major responsibilities you have when you enter your new position is to listen. You listen with your entire being. It's important that you understand you don't have all the answers."

Mary Pat Seurkamp agrees. She says good listening skills are a requisite for the president.

"I think the reason some presidents fail is that they are too far removed from what is going on, too far removed from the students. Most important, they don't spend enough time listening. Good listening skills are essential."

I worked with one president who couldn't stop talking. Being with him was like splashing in a verbal Jacuzzi. He couldn't resist giving his staff his expert opinion on every possible subject.

There was little input at staff meetings and even less discussion. He closed off important opportunities to learn and gain valuable information by expressing his own views too early, and too often. As the psalmist says, he missed "an opportunity to grow in spirit and truth."

The problem is that most people listen to respond, instead of listening to get information. They don't understand that listening is not passive. It requires an immense amount of energy.

One dangerous assumption is that the speaker controls the conversation. Not true! If she is properly probing, asking questions, and listening— she controls the conversation.

Another mistake is thinking that a person begins listening when you start talking. If you believe one of your staff begins listening the moment you begin the conversation, you're mistaken. You also have a problem, if you assume they remember what is most important in what you've said.

Here's the problem when you talk instead of listening. You don't learn anything about the person you're with, their needs and desires. You won't hear any concerns because you're not probing. You're not uncovering any clues to their attitude or what lies below the surface. You don't allow the person to gain any ownership.

If you don't listen, there's not a process for empowerment. You dominate the conversation instead of guiding it.

It gets worse. The spotlight is always on you and not on the other person. When you're talking all the time, you don't give yourself breathing time to think ahead.

You learn by listening to others. You become involved in shaping events rather than having them shape you. You are active and imaginative rather than passive and letting things happen to you.

You maintain a riveting attention on what is occurring and being said. You listen for new ideas. You listen with your total being. You listen with your eyes.

In some of my assignments, I'm called on by a president who feels things aren't going as well as they should. In one situation in a Midwest college, the president felt the senior staff was not operating as a team. There was a total disconnect.

I told the president I would begin by job-shadowing him for the next few days. I sat in a corner and simply observed and listened. I was the fly on the wall. I never said a word (not very easy for a consultant).

A staff person would walk into the office and be seated in front of the president's desk (barrier #1). No warm greeting. Just a nod (#2). The desk was piled high with papers and files. Eye contact was very difficult (#3).

During the conversation, the president was interrupted twice by a phone call. Then there was a mobile phone call— which sounded mostly personal (#4).

While the staff person was talking, the president was leafing through a file. The assistant came in the office and interrupted with some papers that needed to be signed (#5).

On it went. Without letup. One appointment after another.

"There simply isn't time," the president told me after several days of the same scenario. No matter who it was, the president was multi-tasking. Not really listening. During the several days, I was with the president, there happened to be a donor and a trustee who also visited, in addition to staff. Pretty much the same treatment.

I told the president that unless there is a dramatic change, he will be nothing more than an ordinary leader. He heard me, but I'm not certain he listened.

There are those, the really great ones, who never stop listening. I refer to them as *listen-aholics*.

These presidents are ever-alert. They are constantly listening. At work and at play (although there's precious little "play" for the new president). It's the only way possible to learn and to be alerted in advance of unseen problems and exciting new possibilities.

I conducted some informal focus groups. At a recent national meeting of college and university presidents, I wanted to find out from them what they considered the most important attributes and skills of their job. Listening was at the top of the list. The very top.

Think of an electrical cord. Speaking without listening, hearing without listening, is like cutting an electrical cord in two. You plug the one end into a socket, hoping somehow something will light up. But you have broken the connection.

I like the way Thomas Dillon listens. But first, let me describe his office. It is lined with books and religious artifacts. His desk is lined with mountain high piles of unfinished business. Tom is always on the road and typically uses the weekends to catch up. He is, by the way, having wonderful fun. "It's the most exciting job I can imagine."

Visitors are escorted to a corner of the room with soft chairs. Tom's attention is riveted to the person. There are no interruptions. "In case of a fire, let me know."

Tom sits on the edge of his chair most of the time during the session. He is obviously intent on what the visitor is saying. There is extraordinary eye contact. Nodding at the right time. Taking notes. Open questions. Probing. He is a perfect listener.

My own greatest test of listening happened on my first visit with J. Howard Pew. He was for years CEO of the Sun Oil Company (into his 90s) and, of course, the funder of the Pew Trust, one of the most important foundations in the nation.

I was told to be prepared for my visit. I was warned it would not be easy. "Prepare carefully. No fluff. No attempt at humor. No idle conversation. Be precise."

I was indeed prepared. I wrote out my entire presentation and rehearsed it. Several times. This was going to be show time. I was ready.

At two minutes 'til nine, I was ushered into his office. As the grandfather clock in the corner struck nine, two huge center doors of the office opened. In walked Mr. Pew (it is rumored that even his wife called him Mr. Pew). He filled the room.

We sat across from each other, he on a coach and I on a chair facing him. It was that wonderful moment for which I had so carefully prepared. Heart pumping.

"Mr. Pew, I want you to know how pleased and honored I am to have this time with you. You are one of the great corporate leaders of this country and . . ." I was stopped in mid-sentence. The palm of his hand came within inches of my face.

He began. "Thank you very much for coming, Mr. Panas. Now let me tell you about your college." Then ensued over 45 minutes of an uninterrupted review (you wouldn't dare interrupt Mr. Pew) of his analysis of the college I was representing.

It was lacking a few minutes of being ten o'clock when Mr. Pew ended his final sentence. He pulled the pocket watch from his vest, opened the case, and looked at the time.

"This was an immensely interesting conversation," said he. "I appreciate your coming."

The meeting was over. I had said no more than several dozen words. But in so many ways, it was indeed a great conversation. I listened.

You're wondering. Yes, we did get the gift.

Help Others Stand On Tiptoes

"My job is to help others reach their highest aspirations." That's John Hood talking. "When you get right down to it, that's what it's all about."

That's an attribute not often mentioned. It is what I call empowerment. Indeed, that is the objective of a successful president.

There are staff members and faculty on every campus who bring enormous commitment, talent, imagination, and intelligence to their work. The successful president helps motivate a common vision and a common mission. The successful president empowers others to stand on tip-toes to reach lofty objectives.

There is a spark that is ignited that builds into a flame. No wall too high to climb. No problem that can't be overcome. This ability to empower others unleashes a latent talent and an exhilaration for the work of the college.

"I gave careful thought in my early weeks at the university on how to create a climate of high expectations. I wanted fresh ideas that would lead to innovation and change. As much as anything, I wanted to empower others." That's what Joseph White tells me. He goes on.

"I came up with a simple philosophy that I wanted to communicate to everyone in a leadership position at the university. I called it simply, 'the presumption of yes.' What I tried to convey was that no matter the obstacle, it can be done."

The successful president empowers staff to navigate waters they never thought possible.

Here's the problem. You have an overworked staff. They are patching torn sails, plugging leaks, and hoping not to be pitched overboard while rolling from port to starboard.

Keep in mind, you're the captain of this crew. The successful president never forgets it is her job to empower the staff to be the very best they can possibly be.

You have somehow managed to do it. You have whipped this crew into an unbeatable team. It may be best simply to acknowledge the success of this virtually remarkable combination and say, like Dr. Seuss, that it just "happened to happen."

Look Out For the Fat Boy

The failed president didn't keep his attention focused on the priorities. He was weighted down by the emergencies and exigencies.

One of your priorities is to determine which colleges are your competitors. In the changing world of higher education, this should be one of your major concerns. You have probably already discovered that the competition can be fierce.

The successful president never forgets there are other colleges seeking the same students as you. Their literature and Web site is more striking. High school seniors are immediately drawn to them— like steel filings to a magnet.

There are other organizations luring your donors. Their graduate schools, their local hospital, museum, Salvation Army. Their appeal is dramatic and appealing. Urgent, too.

You are struggling to recruit the "right" board members. But so are a dozen other organizations that are going after who you thought were your rightful property. (Remember the five Ws: Work, Wealth, Wisdom, Wallop, and Women.)

The competition for the finest faculty possible (at a salary you can afford) is horrendous. The field is limited. There are a dozen other colleges going after the same small universe of really talented men and women.

You are under-staffed. Your resources are limited. No one is bringing you fresh, exciting ideas. Some competing colleges, as they say, are eating your lunch. They are, as Thoreau described it, "Red in tooth and claw."

The successful president eschews the urgencies that can be passed on to someone else. She rivets her time on the competition and understands what must be done to overcome any possible obstacles. It takes unbounded attention of a fiercely driven person. It takes effort, intensity, and struggle.

The successful president understands that problems are those horrible things you see when you take your eyes off your opportunities. The competition simply becomes one of those opportunities.

It takes creative and strategic thinking, mixed generously with hard work and an intuitive sense of what must be done. Great

thinking gets great results. Mediocre thinking gets mediocre results.

The successful president doesn't know that something can't be
done. He believes God may have been waiting for decades for
someone dumb enough not to know that something couldn't be
done— then he goes ahead and does it.

The failed president doesn't recognize that the competition
is gaining on his college. Or perhaps the college was in a rut when
he became president, and he didn't do anything to make the
necessary changes.

"The fact that it's difficult to see the signs doesn't mean that
they don't exist," said Mark VanDoren. "The signs are there to be
seen. You simply have to be attentive and keep a watchful eye on
the competition."

When Dean Rusk was running the Rockefeller Foundation, he
advised keeping an eye on the Ford Foundation because, "What
the fat boy in the canoe does makes a difference to everybody else."

The successful president understands her college can be as great
as she desires— if she believes in herself, has the courage, determination, dedication, competitive drive, and the will to sacrifice
and pay the price.

The first 120 days. These precious first 120 days. Never again
will you have the same opportunity to make the dramatic impact
and imprint on your college and your presidency as you will in
those first four months.

There will be other issues and extraordinary events in the years
of your tenure that follow that will be memorable. Those early 120
days, however, will set the pace and determine the course you are

about to run in the marathon of your presidency.

I write about the importance of listening in this chapter because it is so under-valued. I describe the need to empower your people and give them ownership. Finally, you need to keep a vigilant eye on the competition. If you do not, the parade will pass you by.

The precious first 120 days. Exhausting, exhilarating. Tenuous, triumphant. Challenges, cheers. Disappointments, dazzling days.

There won't be anything again like those first 120 days. A wild storm, pouring rain. Lightening, thunder. Then suddenly, it's over. "I worked so hard and it went so fast, it all seems like a blur now," Lisa Ryerson tells me.

13

FIRED WITH ENTHUSIASM
(It Didn't Work)

What if it doesn't work out?

What happened? It seemed like a perfect marriage.

The Selection Committee reviewed dozens of resumes. They honed it to a short list of four. You among them.

You returned to the campus for a second visit. This time it was two days of exhausting interviews. The process was working. The Selection Committee finally made a decision. They felt you met their highest hope and expectation.

The Selection Committee invited you to be their new President.

But, it's over. You remember the words of that wonderful song—

Fame,
If you win it—
Comes and goes
In a minute.
Where's the real stuff in life to cling to?

The committee was honest with you. They said the college needed some major changes. They told you it would be like turning the Queen Mary around in the bathtub. But they were certain you could do it.

There needed to be an infusion of funds. You had already shown a good record of raising money.

But that wasn't all. Student enrollment was seriously down and that needed to be punched-up immediately and dramatically.

There's more. The *esprit* among the faculty was at a low ebb. They were without rudder or direction. The committee felt you could motivate them. Raise the academic bar and mold them into an exciting, dedicated team.

The committee was certain you were the answer.

When you took on the engagement, you knew you were taking on a *paseo*, "a walk of death." But you wanted a presidency. You were willing to risk it.

Now, somehow, you have come to that point where both you and the board know you are not going to make it. That once perfect marriage. It happens. It can feel like death by a thousand paper cuts.

Damon Runyon, may have had the answer. He said: "In all human affairs, the odds are always six to five."

There are seven reasons I hear most often that cause an unsuccessful college presidency.

1 STAFF CHANGES One of the major problems I find with college presidents who don't succeed is the failure in the early days to put the right people in the right jobs. Or not to act on staff changes that should be made. I hear this time and time again.

Among those I have worked with and those I interviewed, it is quite clear that the president knows there are some personnel changes that simply must be made. They know there's a problem. They sense that even in the first days. Their inner voice keeps telling them they have got to do something. But they don't.

Good advice is never underestimate your power to change yourself. Or overestimate your power to change others.

2 EXECUTION Here's another reason for failure. The president knew there were problems. He was drowning in them. But he didn't have ideas on how to correct the problem. Or she thought she had a solution, but didn't take the necessary steps to make an immediate and effective change.

Like the deer staring into the headlights of an approaching car, it is impossible for some presidents to move. Execution is a key to a president's success. Failure to act deliberately and decisively is running a race you are destined to lose.

When Kodak ousted Kay Whitmore as CEO, everyone said he failed because he hadn't answered the big question about Kodak's strategy in a digital world.

As a matter of fact, Kodak had created a remarkably aggressive and fail-safe plan to remake itself into a digital imaging company. Whitmore actually embraced the plan enthusiastically.

But somehow, he couldn't move. He had his feet planted firmly in mid-air. He couldn't make it happen. He should have followed the admonition of St. Francis of Assisi: "Let us begin again, for up to now you have done nothing."

Whitmore's strategy was perfect. His intentions were impeccable. But the execution was non-existent. His drive was fixed permanently in neutral.

3 SLAYING THE MESSENGER Some presidents make it clear that they don't like getting bad news. It's not necessarily anything they say. A staff person just knows that problems and trouble are not messages he wants to deliver to the president.

You have to be the kind of president who invites all sorts of information. The good. The bad. But be careful not to slay the messenger.

Even the most successful colleges have bad news. (And some have lots of it) You need to hear it.

Look at it this way. Even though you're totally receptive to hearing the good and the bad— (whatever it is), even those closest to you are sometimes reluctant to give you the bad news. Robert Pritchard says: "The longer I was president at the University of Toronto, the less likely I was to have anyone tell me the unvarnished truth."

4 DECISIVE ACTION I worked with one college where the development officer had missed his financial objective two years before the new president arrived. Then he missed it again the following year, the new president's first year. Obviously, it caused the college serious problems.

Something needed to be done. It required decisive action. But instead of making a change, the president decided he wasn't giving his vice president enough coaching. He resolved to spend more time with him.

The fundraising continued to decline. The vice president had to go. But it was too late. The finances were in a perilous decline. So was the fate of the president.

Being able to execute a program and plan becomes of overriding importance. Perhaps it's fair to say there should be less vision, more execution in the first 120 days. I'll give you an example in corporate life that underlines this issue.

When Lou Gerstner parachuted in to fix the shambles John F. Akers had left at IBM, he famously declared: "The last thing IBM needs right now is a vision. We have plenty of that. We need to focus on decisiveness and we need to simplify the organization for speed in decision making. We need to break the gridlock."

He could have said that of some failed presidencies in higher education.

I worked with a college in the Southwest that had been suffering severely with admissions. Each year more than the year before. What was needed was decisive action. Instead, the new president was frozen in place.

He called in a consultant to study the issue (six months), someone to analyze demographics (one month), focus groups with high school counselors (three months), focus groups with high school seniors (two months), and then a market research study (four months). Henry Ford once said if we had done market research and asked the public what they wanted, they would have told us: "Faster Horses."

The president lost a valuable year. Created an even more severe financial crunch. Perpetuated great damage to the spirit on the campus. Worse, caused a lack of confidence in his leadership.

He fired the entire admissions team the following year. Applications increased 120 percent.

5 TAKE CARE OF YOUR PEOPLE The best presidents never hesitate to fire when they must. But there's something more important. A larger point is that you must be deeply interested in your people. You must show it. No one cares how much you know until they know how much you care.

Joseph White says: "As large as the university is, I know all our key people. I care about them. I want them to succeed. I want them all to feel like winners. A leader cares about his people."

Jack Welch said: "I have an inscription on my office wall. It says: 'People first. Vision and strategy second.'"

6 LACK OF PERSONAL SKILLS I spoke recently with the chair of a college board. She told me they had to remove the president (after his first academic year).

"It wasn't that he didn't have great vision. He did. He certainly knew higher education. He was quite an academician. His credentials were sterling.

"His personal relations were horrible. He had no skill with people. He managed to upset everyone. Complaints were flying at us from everywhere. I tried to counsel with him several times in the early months, but to no avail."

It's not really "an ability to deal with people." That smacks of managing, directing down.

What you're really after is a sensitivity and genuine empathy for people. Part of it, I believe, is loving your job as president and loving your people.

It means getting to know them and learning what's inside their minds and heart. That's what I mean when I refer to personal skills— being sensitive and empathetic to all in the college community.

Here's what Peter Drucker says about leadership.

"Leadership is about competency, ability to inspire, and people skills. The college has no physical product other than its students. That is why I feel skill in dealing with people may be the most important attribute of the president."

7 GO AHEAD— DECIDE Effective college presidents drive decisions, not delay them.

You feel overwhelmed with how much must be done. Putting out fires, being everywhere, making the necessary contacts, visiting with the right people.

Everyone wants a piece of you— board members, staff, faculty, students, and of course, the attorneys who are suing. You feel you are being nibbled to death by ducks.

Where does the time go? Who has time to think? Dream? You feel people don't believe you're doing any work— but they don't understand how hard it is to move a big pile of sand with a pair of tweezers.

Even with all you have to do and in the midst of fires igniting all around you, as the president— you must be capable of decisive and non-deferred decision-making. You do all this while focusing on the objective of the college— that is to achieve the highest aspirations possible for your students.

Harvard Business School teaches its students that whether they decide yes or they decide no— they will be right 80 percent of the time. The great failure is in delaying the decision.

Some things that are wrong, if left alone, will right themselves. Some things, no matter what you do, cannot be righted. Most things, if you make a prompt decision can be made right.

The lesson is: Go ahead. Just make a decision. The failed president will never consider changing his position. Just finding one is enough of a challenge for him.

I loved watching Peter Armacost in action. At the time, he was president of Eckerd College. At the end of a meeting with the staff, when he asked them to collect data and think about a problem that required a decision, he would grab a pen and start writing.

He's noting exactly what is supposed to be done, by whom, and when. Before the meeting is about to close, he reviews those notes with all of the assignments. Then he sends a memo nailing down the assignment. He reminds the staff they will be asked for input regarding the decision.

At the next meeting, he goes around the room and asks everyone's opinion. He doesn't ask for or expect consensus. Peter understands the ultimate decision is his. Peter is a disciple of Harry Truman's dictum: If you can't stand the heat, get out of the kitchen.

"Don't boil the ocean" means don't try to analyze everything. The successful president doesn't have time to doubt or postpone a decision. There is a quality of "certainty."

The failed president, when faced with a decision practices: Ready-Aim…Aim…Aim— and never fires.

The indecisive president reminds me of the three men who were shown a room with two doors. They were told that behind one door was wealth beyond their dreams— gold, silver, priceless jewels. Behind the other door was a hungry man-eating tiger.

They were each given the option of entering the room and opening a door. The first man refused the choice and left.

The second man— a strong believer in strategic planning— hauled out his computer, analyzed probability data, performed some risk examinations, diagrammed graphs, conducted a SWAT analysis, produced charts, created worst-case scenarios, plotted a reliability abstract, developed a matrix for benchmarking, and conducted an opportunity analysis. After much deliberation, he opened a door and was eaten by a low-probability man-eating tiger.

The third man (of course, the third one is always the winner) spent his time learning to tame tigers.

It can be tough. Some decisions have such ripple-ramifications. The hotter the fire, the tougher the metal.

So there you are. You've been told the board is not going to renew your contract. You feel like Catherine's comment in the devastating ending of A Farewell to Arms, "It's such a dirty trick."

Or worse, you have been asked to "resign"— as the newspaper reports about your departure, "to seek other career opportunities and spend more time with the family."

You were asked to a party, and now you're sitting out the dance. To paraphrase Cole Porter, What a swell party it's been.

It's painful. Plenty. But time helps heal. The Bible tells us, though we weep through the night, joy will come in the morning.

Take some comfort. You're in good company. Gordon Gee had an outstanding record at Ohio State University. He went from there to Brown University— where he was fired. Then to Vanderbilt University— where he was fired.

Gee then returned to Ohio State as president, where at his first meeting with the faculty they gave him a standing ovation to welcome him home.

Gee told the faculty: "The only other time I ever received a standing ovation from the faculty was when the Chairman of the Board of Vanderbilt announced at the Faculty Senate that I had been fired." To paraphrase Clark Kerr, he took on the job with great enthusiasm . . . and was fired the same way.

It isn't pleasant. When you come to the end of your rope, tie a knot in it and hang on. You feel like ranting, *l'haudil*, like Job, at the injustice of it all and demanding an accounting by God.

This isn't the end. T.S. Elliot said, "In the end is my beginning." You will go on to great things. This isn't your whole book. Only a chapter.

14

BRAVO! YOU MADE IT
(The Path to A Successful Tenure)

Congratulations. You have gone beyond the magic 120 days. You are on your way to an exciting and successful tenure.

I give you permission to celebrate your achievement by beginning with a *triple pirouette* and ending with an arabesque on the floor. Just like Mikhail Baryshnikov.

You took a lesson from Greek Mythology about Proteus, the old man of the sea. He escaped his captors by assuming all sorts of shapes.

As Mark Twain said, "You surprised everybody, and astounded the rest." You made it! I hear in the background the resounding impact of Tchaikovsky's *1812 Overture*.

James Johnson understands there is no perfect job. There is travail and turmoil along with the excitement and exhilaration.

"There were days that were tortuous," James says. "I know I'm no superman. But I'll tell you what got me through. I know some-one wanted me to be at Ohio Valley. It was ordained."

It's important to remember it's not a sprint. Your tenure at the college is a long run. You have much to accomplish. Like the marathon, there will be some struggles along the way.

You will find some duties which are onerous in the years ahead. If not immediately, they will be eventually. Your success depends not merely on how well you do things you enjoy, but how persistently and devotedly you perform those duties you don't.

Most of the months ahead, you will feel much like Jake Schrum.

"I think there's no greater opportunity than being a college president. You are preparing the next generation. It's a challenge, but a wonderful opportunity. What else could you do that's more rewarding. There's nothing quite like it."

Leonardo Da Vinci is one of history's greatest thinkers and doers. He developed some principles which are curiously appro-priate for today's college president. They are a beautiful and help-ful guide for your future years. The Da Vincian Principles you should practice are:

Curiosità— An insatiably curious approach to life and an un-relenting quest for continuous learning.

Dimostrazione— A commitment to test knowledge through experience, persistence, and a willingness to learn from mistakes.

Sensazione— The continual refinement of the senses and skills, as the means to enliven experience.

Sfumato (literally "Going up in Smoke")— A willingness to embrace ambiguity, paradox, and uncertainty.

Arte/Scienza— The development of the balance between science and art, logic and imagination. "Whole-brain" thinking.

Corporalita— The cultivation of grace, fitness, and poise.

Connessione— A recognition of and appreciation for the interconnectedness of all things and phenomena. Systems thinking.

"To make a living is no longer enough," said Peter Drucker. "Work also has to make a life." But what a wonderful life you have ahead of you in your years as a college president.

To paraphrase *Flaubert, the life of a college president can be hell. It is a dog's life. But the only one worth living. You suffer more. You're frustrated more by things that don't seem to bother other people. But you also live so much more. You live so much more intensely and so much more vitally. And with so much more of a sense of meaning, of consequentiality. Everything matters. You become hooked. You are hooked more deeply than any narcotics addict could possibly be on heroin. But being a college president is life-giving.*

Talk about it being life-giving, listen to Lisa Marsh Reyerson.

"It's funny. I knew the moment I put the key in my office door on the very first day that I was deeply honored. That's when I really thought for the very first time what a privilege it was being president."

It is quite true that what we love to do, we do well. Having done it well, we wish to do it even better. You will find this to be true. You will even enjoy the long hours and be driven by action. You will have this desire to be at the top of your game and achieve wondrous things for your college and your vision for the future.

"I am passionate about the college," says Sue DeWine. "I love my work. I love it!" I heard that from all of the presidents.

As a matter of fact, if you don't get up every morning blessing the day ahead and looking forward to your work, something is the matter. It ought to be fun. Tom Dillon agrees.

"Except for four hours of sleeping, I worked every hour of every day in those early months. But it wasn't really work. The college is my passion. Every day was fun."

I believe if you're not feeling wondrous joy and unending fulfillment in the work, something's wrong. You should be one with Einstein who said: "The first two hours at the job I consider to be hard work and drudgery. The next 12 hours are just plain fun."

Buck Smith (Davis & Elkins College) told me that even if he wasn't paid for doing what he does, he would keep doing it free. (Actually, he does.) For him, being a college president is both his job and his avocation.

For the college president who is most effective, it's an exhilarating journey, a ministry brimming with rewards and fulfillment. I am convinced that if it isn't a great joy for you, you are perhaps not in the right position. Or at the right college.

Steve Jobs (Apple Computers) received an honorary degree from Stanford University. In his acceptance speech, he said: "The only way to do great work is to love what you do. If you're not passionate and love your job, do something else."

It should be a joy. Every morning (well, most mornings!) should be like the refrain from the 1960 popular song: "What A

Day For A Daydream." In the years ahead, you will exude an excitement, a sense of life, a reach, and hope to an extent that's hard to describe.

As Antony says in Shakespeare's *Antony & Cleopatra:* "This is the business we love, and we rise at sunrise and go to it with delight."

I keep referring to the joy. Obviously, it won't always be that way. There will be times you will feel like one of the brothers in *Beau Gest,* the 1939 French Foreign Legion film, where they touch each other to see if they're still alive.

There are days that may look bleak. Your job as president is to inspire all in the college by your faith and hope. You take the setbacks in your stride. You talk about all the gains, not the losses. The victories, not the problems.

You pursue your vision and dreams for the college. Ah, yes, there can actually be joy, some days, in the struggle. It requires your endurance, determination, and unending spirit.

The pressure in the job can be fierce. I'm reminded that a diamond is a chunk of coal that made good under pressure.

The years ahead will be a high adventure. Success is the result of having the hunger, the courage, and the will to be the best you can be. It's wonderful fun to do the impossible.

"I am a cockeyed optimist. I don't know where I'm going," said Carl Sandburg, "but I'm on my way." There will be days like that for you.

You will work long, you will work hard, you will work joyfully. You will be your very best. Nothing less will do. When you reach this zenith, you will be able to say, "I have found my hero, and he is me."

President Ronald Reagan said life is a fast moving train. You want to grab on and hold on and enjoy the feel of the wind in your hair. Enjoy the ride. It's ungrateful not to do so.

In becoming president, you heard the anthem of the call. You had, from the earliest of time, as the deepest thing within you, believed you were being kept for something rare and strange that was sooner or later to happen to you.

Your years ahead will be successful. But heed the words of Bill Gates: "Success is a lousy teacher. It seduces smart people into thinking they can't lose. I'm not good on self-congratulations. The more successful I am, the more vulnerable I feel. When you do well, people expect even better next time around."

Continue to have faith in yourself. Create the kind of person you will be happy to live with all of your life. I have eight Principles I pass on to you. Much of this, in a way, is the tapestry of what was woven during my visits.

1   Have fun. Have a ball with everything you do and with the people around you.

2   Be passionate about what you do. Have it burn like fire in your bones.

3   Believe you can do it. Be positive. If you feel there are things that can't be done, you stand a good chance of being a prophet. If you believe you can, you can. If you believe you can't, you won't.

4   Make your own luck. The better you are prepared, the luckier you will be.

5   Be courageous. Don't be afraid to fail. Michael Jordan said that the only baskets he did not make were the shots he didn't take.

6   If you do fail, figure out why— and try again. Failing is no disgrace. The great failure is in not trying again.

7   Don't take *no* for an answer. *No* sometimes means maybe, or not yet, or try again.

8   Get a dream. Dream, Decide, Dare, Do.

You have chosen what Martin Amis calls, "The wonderful eligibility to be noble." You recognize in yourself one who is not nearly arrived, but remains a learner. You must continue to seek, probe, examine. You are in a constant state of becoming. You continue to grow.

In the years ahead, regard yourself as a person in process. There is no end to the challenge of being a college president— the excitement, the curiosity, and the wonder.

You have now successfully completed the first 120 days. All the years in front of you will be packed with glorious achievement. Like the Apostle Paul, you will say, "I have fought the good fight, I have finished the race, and I have remained faithful."

Lucky you. You have managed to grab the Brass Ring and accepted an invitation to life's most exciting party. The years ahead will bow to you. You will be remembered. Your name will be like a thoroughbred's, a horse that ran and won.

15

THE TENETS
(Pledging Your Success)

*"There are three irrefutable rules which will assure
your success as a president. Unfortunately, no one
has ever discovered what they are."*
John Lewis Russell

Is there a *presidential type?* Outgoing, people-oriented, extremely well organized, a brilliant academic, a change-agent, a leader. A combination of Mother Theresa and Jack Welch.

It is really difficult, perhaps impossible, to know what makes an ideal president. If you were designing the perfect flycatcher, you probably wouldn't design it to look like a frog.

I am at once struck with the great diversity among the presidents I interviewed for this book. They are tall and short, men and women, young and not so young, thin and stocky, mellow and fierce. They certainly do not fit any simple cookie-cutter mold.

In my interviewing, and from all I heard and know, there is one central converging theme that impressed me most of all. I heard it in every visit I made.

All of the presidents tell me that the first 120 days of their presidency are the most demanding and draining of all of their years in the role. They are also the most exciting and exhilarating.

Each person was quite clear that the road to success in their presidency was paved during those first 120 days. Some were fairly new in their office and one is in his fourth presidency. The refrain, however, was the same.

The first 120 days establish the pattern. Success or not so successful.

I discovered a simple fact. There probably are no gimmicks or tricks. No road signs that can direct you precisely down the path of success. No yellow brick road to Oz.

In this book, I try to light the way. I give you some road signs to help provide direction.

What I offer now, in this chapter, are some observations, factors, and findings that will ensure your success. These are the verities of a successful president I described in earlier chapters. In a more abbreviated form I review now what must be done during your early months. These are canons to work by. Tenets you can count on. A roadmap you are to follow.

1. The course is set. The first 120 days you are in office determines the success of your presidency. Or…well, let's face it—your failure. It is essential you use those early months to propel you to a rewarding and fulfilling presidency.

The effective president chooses to succeed. You don't stumble on success. You choose it. It happens in the first 120 days.

2. All your actions count. It is essential in the early days to think carefully about your actions, your meetings, your speeches, and all your activities. Everything you do on and off the campus. Each day and on weekends. All of the faculty and staff, the alumni, and your board are watching and waiting. Even the students. There's no other time you will be under such intense scrutiny.

3. Make or break time. If you're getting ready to run a marathon, you spend a lot of time before the race preparing. It's the same in becoming a new president. The time between your selection and when you actually take office is the most important period to help you prepare for the new position.

Before your arrival, you should understand the challenges of your new post and be thinking about the opportunities. Thinking and planning.

4. Understand the objectives. Before you take office, it's important to know what specific objectives the board would like to have you achieve during your presidency. This is something you should discuss in the early meetings, even before you are officially selected.

Once you become the successful candidate, the board needs to let you know what their hopes are for your work and what some of the top priorities are for the college.

If the board doesn't initiate this, you should. Let them know what your understanding is of their hopes and primary objectives for the future.

This should be in writing as a matter of record. It will be important in evaluating your progress. It is the document that ensures there is no ambiguity about what is urgent and imperative.

5. Make certain there's an employee agreement. Before you begin your new position, you need to make certain there is an agreement both you and the board have negotiated and agreed upon. This should not be a simple matter of understanding but rather a written and signed document.

6. Select a mentor. Enlist a mentor or a small network of advisers you regard highly— those you can count on when you hit a blank wall. That will happen. It is a crime of over-confidence to feel you can take on this job entirely on your own. Chances are almost certain you won't be able to confide fully in anyone on the campus.

7. A transition committee helps. It is important that a special group be appointed at the college that assists in making the transition from the old to the new. The chair of the committee should be in regular contact with you to keep you apprised of plans.

This is the group that plans for the media announcement of your selection. The committee arranges all of the early meetings you will have on campus where you will greet some of your most important constituencies. It is possible, also, to arrange for alumni meetings in key cities during your early four months.

8. Read everything. Have the college send you everything possible that will help you prepare for your arrival. Everything. This includes historical documents, bylaws, minutes of past board meetings, and all publications.

You also need to have financial statements from past years, a roster of all board members, an organization chart of your staff, and all other information that can possibly help get you off to a running start.

If there has been a recent Accreditation, review all of the documents that were prepared for that. Be certain to read the Report from the visiting accrediting team.

9. Be certain you ask. There will be no other time quite like this in helping you prepare for your first day. You are the new president and you have a right to know everything possible about the situation. Be comfortable in asking for any information you feel will be helpful. Your genius and success is your infinite capacity for taking pains in advance of moving to the campus.

10. You learn as you go along. No matter how effective a job you do in preparing, you can't learn everything right away. The good news is, you don't need to. You are a learning-animal in the first 120 days. Probing. Asking. Listening. Learning.

In the first three or four months, you begin to understand the thrum and rhythm of the campus. The culture. The way the staff reacts to each other, the pecking order, the college politics.

No matter how carefully you prepared, financial statements and board minutes won't give much of a clue to the culture and the order of things. Eric Hoffer, in his book *The True Believer*, wrote: "We can be absolutely certain only about the things we don't yet understand."

11. Enjoy the presidency. As you begin your early days in office, make certain it's fun. You will work hard and long hours— but it will be worth it. You are the president, the leader— whether in the early days the office fits comfortably or not. Soon it will be a joy. You will be writing psalms of passion and celebration.

12. Be curious and daring. Be prepared in those first 120 days to take risks, experiment, attend to new things, and make changes.

"Work hard, take chances, be very bold," says a character in the movie Julia. Even in those early days, especially in those early days, have a healthy impatience and discontent with anything less than zenith performance.

13. Keep a proper balance. You will have a tremendous amount to accomplish in your first 120 days. It's quite likely you will never again be under such intense pressure. Keep in mind that your presidency is a series of short spirits. Be certain to find time to just think. Relax as much as you can. Take deep breaths!

You will find it takes a blazing versatility and balance. There is a ferocious appetite for information and an unending assimilation of learning. You must be a person of action. At the same time you must have an opportunity to just reflect. Dream.

In all your frantic darting and dashing— take some time-outs to simply reflect. It is the space between the notes that makes the music.

14. Meetings with senior staff are important. You will want to meet with your senior staff individually and as a group in your first few days, and then regularly after that. Depending on the situation, you will want to meet with your senior staff at least once a week and in some cases, even more often than that.

15. Take measure. These early days will give you an opportunity to evaluate your senior staff. Very early on, you may decide that one or two don't quite measure up. You hope for a team that is as excited about the potential and is as eager to move the college forward as you are. Sadly, this doesn't always happen.

You may feel that someone on the staff is not going to make it.

Take action quickly. Every president I spoke with indicated that their only disappointment in this regard is that they didn't take the necessary action sooner. They knew from almost the first weeks that changes had to be made. They all regretted they didn't act sooner.

16. What you look for. You look for a senior staff that is confident, optimistic, and audacious. You hope for a detonation of ideas. You want to make certain they understand your objectives, what you want to achieve, and how you like to work with staff. You let them know it's going to be collaborative— but in a circumspect way, it becomes clear you are in charge.

17. Build momentum. If there is a lack of energy in your early weeks, the college community perceives it. Your job is to demonstrate dynamic leadership. Everyone is watching. Waiting. Seek some early visible victories. You are the college's hope, vision, and vitality.

18. It's lonely. You will find it lonely at the top. There's really no one you can talk with or confide in. At times, it is even difficult to talk with the chair of your board. It may be awkward to let him know there are some situations that are puzzling and you don't have an easy answer. That's one of the major reasons to have a mentor you can confide in.

19. You are the model. You symbolize the college's vision and future. You carry the message. Your impact in the first 120 days is without bounds. Everyone is measuring your passion and commitment. It will be infectious and they will follow.

20. Don't worry about stumbling. It will happen. There will be times things don't work out as you had planned. There will be days you will be mumbling the old Cheyenne-warrior cry: "It is a good day to die."

You cannot let down, you don't know defeat, you are unflap-pable. You are the president, the music-maker, the dreamer of dreams.

In your job, there will be blips. It may be one of your decisions. They won't all be popular. Or it may be your dazzling speech that turned out to be as flat as the floor in your gymnasium. Or a horrible first impression with the college's largest donor.

It's probably not as bad as you thought. It's what Eric Hoffer, the philosopher-longshoreman turned-writer, called, "Things which are not, and tomorrow will be forgotten." You did your very best.

When he left the presidency, Harry Truman was asked for what achievement he was most proud. "I did the very best I could, at that given time, with all the talent and energy possible I could muster."

21. Be curious. One of the most important factors in a suc-cessful 120 days is to be curious about everything around you. You remain inquisitive, ask questions, probe.

You read everything. You observe, you walk the campus, talk to students, and visit with faculty.

You are a curiosity-seeker. You have a certain rash, restless curiosity, like a sort of Ulysses.

22. Be positive. Decide exactly what you want and what you are determined to achieve in the first 120 days. Write down your objectives. If you can conceive it, you can achieve it.

When you make your list, the long roster may seem daunting.

But you don't mind. Make the list of objectives with target dates. If you don't put it in writing, it's like tennis without the net.

23. There is only one thing that counts. Keep in mind, with all going on around you and with the frantic pace you are maintaining— there is only one thing that really counts. Your ultimate responsibility is to make certain you are providing the most effective education possible in helping your students reach their highest aspirations. It's all about the students.

24. Don't plan on a lot of sleep. Shakespeare had you in mind when he wrote in *Hamlet:* "Twenty-hours a day, he is a thinking, working being." In those early days, you will find your days filled with all sorts of meetings, calls that have to be made, contacts you can't miss, speeches you have to give, and activities you have to attend.

You hope for a 28-hour day. There will be times you will feel like Atlas, bowed down beneath a burden that cracks the bones and solidifies the blood.

You may find that there aren't more than four or five hours of sleep before you have to begin the day again. You identify with Faubert who said: "Everyday I go from exhaustion to a state of collapse." But you will find it's fun and exhilarating.

In the end, that's what you will love about being president. You never say goodbye to the excitement or the challenge.

25. Spend time with the board. It's important you meet with all board members within the first few weeks. It's best if you can do this one-on-one. Failing that, perhaps because of the distance and your own time limitations, you may have to do it by telephone.

Let them know how you are settling in and some of the

extraordinary opportunities you are uncovering. It's also an excellent time to let them know about your early vision for the future.

26. Meet with donors. There is a small number, very likely no more than 20 sources, who represent the major philanthropy of the college. There may be some, also, who may not be your largest donors but are men and women who are of significant influence to the college.

In the first 120 days, you should make contact with them. They will want to take measure of their new leader. They will want to know how bright the flame burns. Have as much information as possible about each of these people before you make the call.

27. Take advantage of the honeymoon. There is something special about the first 120 days. Your board and major donors are more willing than ever to provide what you feel must be done in order to make the dream a reality. Resources, staffing, equipment, whatever you need.

This is the best time possible to ask. Be bold. (Remember Scott Miller asking for $50 million his first meeting— and getting it.) It's their college. They are counting on you to tell them what must be done.

28. Students count. You will be torn. You need to take as much time as you possibly can meeting with students. That's what it's all about. That's why you became president. Even with all of the contacts that you must make with donors, board members, and faculty— don't neglect the students.

Walk the campus, go to the cafeteria, attend student activities, be everywhere. Ben Franklin said that's what is important: "Connect. Just connect."

29. Make the necessary decisions. You will be faced with major decisions that have to be made. And minor ones, too. Decide. Don't delay. Don't wait for a consensus or count on getting one. Get as much input as you possibly can. But the final decision is yours.

What's interesting is that Business Schools tell us that in 80% of the situations, it doesn't matter whether you decide *yes* or *no*. The important thing is that you decide.

30. Trust your impulses. There are times when you have collected all the data you possibly can. You've spoken with every appropriate person that's relevant to the situation. You're still not certain. That won't be unusual. That's when you trust your impulses.

You were chosen to be president because you are precisely the right person. Your intuitive hunch, the vision that comes to you in a flash, is most often the right thing to do. Go with it.

31. Don't degrade the past. No matter how bad you find the situation, (in some cases you may even find the college teetering), do not dwell on the past. Play the cards you've been dealt as best you can. The college community will be looking to you for your leadership, your vision, and your hopes for the future. That's where to place your emphasis. Don't demean the past in any way. Speak in the future tense.

32. Honor your predecessor. No matter what, pay due respect to the person you follow. Someone will be taking your place someday. You may feel you have inherited a mess. Just remember as Paul McCartney would sing, "I've got to admit it's getting better," John Lennon would chime in, "Because it can't get much worse."

33. Have a smooth transition. Make certain you have a smooth transition from the old to the new. But it need not be a long one. A few days is normally sufficient time to make the bridge. Then if you need any help, or if there are questions to be asked of your predecessor, sometime in the future you can do that when it's necessary. Make certain there is a warm, cordial, and grateful relationship.

Trustees often think a long transition is necessary. I haven't found this to be needed or beneficial. In fact, it's been awkward and unnecessarily time-consuming— when time is so precious. Here's the answer: Take as much time as you need for the transition. No more.

34. Consider a break. It is most often a good idea that there be a considerable time-separation from the old to the new. This is something most effectively worked out by the board after you have been selected. There should be those few days, or whatever time is necessary, to make the transition. Then the former president should be off campus for some time— except perhaps to attend a very special occasion.

Laurence McKinley Gould was the much revered president at Carleton College who retired after 26 extremely successful years. The board wanted him to stay on as chancellor. He declined because he knew it would inhibit his successor. At the very hour of his going-away retirement luncheon (700 in attendance), the movers had just finished packing his household goods for another state. Gould and his wife got in the car and drove off. Never to return.

35. Chancellor? Or not? There are times that the board will consider naming the former president as chancellor. This pays honor to someone who has served with great distinction and a long tenure.

It serves no purpose, however, to do this unless there are specific objectives for the chancellor to meet, duties that should be performed. Most often this is done for fundraising. But if the former president hasn't been raising major funds in the past, there is no reason to expect this will be done in the future.

The naming of the former president as chancellor is something that should be cleared with the new president before the engagement is official. If it is to be done, and you agree, make certain there are specific objectives, time limitations imposed of some sort, and an understanding that the chancellor reports to you.

Your predecessor must not serve on the board. Must not. Period.

36. Keep in contact with the board chair. From the time you are selected until you actually move on the campus, it's a good idea to keep in some sort of regular contact with your board chair. Obviously, don't be a pest— but casual conversations are helpful and important.

Once you are on the job, keep in contact with the chair, perhaps once a week for the first several months. This is an important way to keep the chair posted on how things seem to be going, to respond to any questions you might have, and talk about all of the great things that are happening on campus. It's all right to share some concerns, but it's helpful to be upbeat and positive.

Be sensitive. You will sense if you're calling too often.

37. Board meetings are your time to shine. Obviously, all of the board meetings you have during your presidency are important. But your first official meeting with trustees sets the stage for all that follow.

Make certain your first meeting is very well scripted. Prepare carefully. Go over the agenda in detail with the chair to make certain things are perfectly in place.

You are on stage. It's your time to shine. That's important. I also like to have the president's report come early or even first on the agenda. It doesn't get the regard and attention that's due if it's last.

Try reporting first on the agenda the first year or so. See how it goes. If you hear someone say, "but we've never done it that way before"— that's the best reason for doing it.

38. Trustees are the college's future. This is the most important time possible to let trustees know, in your individual sessions with them, how vital they are to the future of the college. You need not be hesitant about telling them that you are counting on them.

You may discover there were a few who were not roaring advocates of yours at first, but finally came around to your selection. These trustees are all the more important for you to win over. Work on it.

Keep raising the bar for your trustees. Let them know what's expected. (Better still, have the chair let them know.) Trustees will stand on tip-toes to meet high standards, but only if they know what is expected.

39. There mustn't be a deficit. Everyone is concerned about a financial deficit. Borrowing. Dipping into the endowment. Chances are this is where you will be giving a great deal of attention in your early days.

But there's something even more important than a financial

deficit and balancing your budget. That's a *Mission Deficit*.

It's the responsibility of the board to secure sufficient funds to meet your mission. It's their job to role up their sleeves and make certain there are sufficient funds to reach your institutional aspirations. That's more consequential than just simply balancing your budget.

Allowing a *Mission Deficit* will ultimately be the spiritual demise of the college, its loss of heart and soul.

40. There should be an evaluation. It is important that you have an understanding with the chair that there will be an evaluation of your work after an early period. Perhaps after the first six months. That's a good time to make an assessment of your early days, determine whether the initial objectives and priorities were appropriate and are being met, and take a look at the next six months.

I had suggested earlier that when you are first selected, the board presents you with a written description of what they feel are the items most important for your immediate and priority attention. Your success with these imperatives should be measured.

This can be an unnerving exercise. The objectives may not have been realistic. Perhaps you should have challenged them. But how could you know for certain. This demonstrates yet again the wisdom of the late jazz pianist, Fats Waller whose endearing phrase, "one never knows, do one?" seems uncommonly appropriate here.

You may feel it was like driving from the high board. But you see opportunities where others see only what can't be done. You are willing to take great risks because you know the returns will be great.

41. You get the kind of board you deserve. Having a truly effective board determines the vitality and future of the college. Many colleges get the kind of board they deserve (by not recruiting effectively) rather than the kind of board that they must have. As the president, you are the coach in helping recruit the trustees you should. It is up to you to settle for nothing less than the very best.

You need the kind of board that men and women strive to be on. There should be a certain caché about being one of your trustees.

42. Aim high. In recruiting new board members, consider the 5 Ws— Work, Wealth, Wisdom, Wallop, Women. If you are willing to settle for less than the best, that's the kind of board you will end up with— less than the best.

43. The holy canon. An important truth that will help in much of the activity in your position as the new president is that: "You will be hurt more by those who would have said *yes* but weren't asked— than by those who say *no*." Let that be your credo.

I consider this a sacred verity. So much so I suggest you have it typed on a 3x5 card, laminated, and then placed in your desk's middle drawer so you see it every day. Or put it on the desktop screen on your computer.

Don't say no for anyone. This is important counsel whether you are seeking a new board member, going after a large gift, or trying to recruit an important person for the faculty.

44. It's a magic partnership. You need to say to the trustees: "I work for you, but I can't do it without you. I need your help." You need their participation and commitment. Let them know it's the only way you can be an effective president. You can't do it alone.

It is a partnership. When it works effectively, it's a magic partnership.

45. Go for the best. Regarding your senior staff, if you are willing to settle for a middling, mediocre team— that's probably what you will get. Run of the mill staff, uninspired ideas, and incompetent work.

You mustn't settle for adequate or average. Good isn't good enough. You want the kind of staff James Russell Lowell wrote about: "What they dare to envision in their wildest dreams, they dare to do."

46. Some qualities to look for. In considering a senior staff person, first of all seek a person whose values and character are in complete congruity with yours and the college's. Then look for uncommon competency to do the job (experience may not be as important as you think). Search for self-confidence, a hunger to win, and a desire to do more than is expected. If you get all of that— you have a winner. You won the staff lottery.

47. Ignite the spark. You want to infuse the senior staff with your own passion. They need to know your insistent commitment to success and understand your vision for the future. Your excitement and enthusiasm are contagious. You light the fire.

48. Let them know. It's essential that you let the senior staff know in the early weeks who you are, what you are about, and what you expect. It's up to you. You can make and shape your conditions, environment, and the destiny of your presidency.

Tell them how you like things done and what it's like working with you. Be certain to let them know the sorts of things that you find upsetting. They shouldn't have to figure out on their own what it will be like working with you. Or have to guess.

49. Give them hope. No matter how good a situation you find when you assume office, it's important you let all the constituencies of your college community know of your mighty desires and heroic goals for the future. Give everybody hope.

That's what your trustees, staff, and faculty are expecting from you. A future with promise and towering aspirations. Give them confidence, faith, and heart. Give them hope.

Spread the word. Let everyone know. The college is reaching for the stars.

50. Eschew the word *can't*. On a pretty regular basis, you will be hearing "we tried that before," "it won't work here," "it's not in our budget," "it can't be done." Count on it. You'll be hearing those phrases.

Put your foot down. Tell folks you will not tolerate any more negatives. You don't want to hear about what can't be done. You want your team to tell you how to make it happen. Not can't, but how.

Bonnie McElveen Hunter is chair of the board of the American Red Cross. That's virtually a full-time volunteer job. She spends 90 percent of her time doing that. She also owns and runs a multi-million dollar business. That takes the other 90% of her time!

When she was five years old, growing up in Bossier City (Louisiana), her mother, Madeline, took Bonnie and her sister into the backyard. She had a shoebox, two pieces of paper, and two pencils.

Madeline told the two young girls to dig a deep hole. Next, she told them to write the word *can't* on the paper and put their sheets in the shoebox. Then she had them bury the shoebox.

"Now you see," Madeline said, "the word *can't* is buried, buried forever. You will never be able to use the word again."

Next meeting of your Senior Staff, tell them to bring a shoe-box.

51. Ask for input. Everyone knows the final decision is ultimately yours. But absorb as much input as you possibly can. You are a sponge soaking up information. Some staff may not always agree with you. Cherish that. Those who wholeheartedly agree and those who disagree are equally important.

Particularly in the early days, you will be faced with wrenching decisions you may have to make. The successful president sees these as great opportunities— brilliantly disguised as impossible situations.

It is possible that your decision is such that you stand virtually alone. Almost naked. Hawthorne makes us aware of, "how thin is the weave that hides our nakedness, how fragile the fabric."

52. Good working relationship. What you wish for in your staff is a good relationship, a close working association, and mutual respect. Don't worry about being a friend. In fact, there seems to be evidence that a intimate relationship can be a negative. The key probably is: Warm, cordial, empathetic, understanding— but not close friends.

53. The faculty is everything. You can have beautiful buildings, the latest in equipment, and a sparkling campus. These are all important. But if you don't have a truly effective faculty, you won't have an outstanding college. John Dewey once described

the most effective education possible is a great teacher and a
student sitting side-by-side on a log.

54. You are the faculty's advocate. You are the major cheerleader for the faculty. You lead the parade.

You preach the gospel: to teach, to guide, to nurture, to
inspire— these are life's noblest attainments.

The faculty understands that you are on their side. You are
willing to do whatever you can in order to provide the greatest
education possible for the students.

There are times, however, the faculty needs to be reminded
that you are the president. The leader. That in no way diminishes
the fact you and the faculty are bonded by an unwavering dedication that your greatest motivation is the singular opportunity to
make a difference.

55. Faculty access can be a problem. It can happen easily,
and often unconsciously. Some of the trustees know the faculty
quite well, particularly board members who have been around a
long time. Some of the trustees may have actually been taught by
some of the faculty when they were students at the college.

But it is important that faculty do not have access to trustees
on matters of the college. It needs to be made clear to trustees that
if they hear from any faculty regarding an issue about the college
or president, it should be directed to the chairman of the board.

56. Talk with the faculty. In your first few weeks, meet with
as many faculty as possible— individually and in groups. You will
certainly want to meet individually with all your department and
division heads.

The early days provide an excellent opportunity to get to

know them well, and hear what their objectives are for the college and their work. You listen. It's important, also, that they get to know you and what you are all about. They need to hear your objectives.

57. Nothing more important. The faculty is at the very front line of your college. Nothing is more important than a faculty that is passionate about the college, captures your commitment and vision for the future, and is willing to do whatever is necessary to create a transformational environment for the students.

Here's what is essential. The faculty represents the college— its history, its mission, and its spirit. Presidents come and go. So do students. The faculty, by and large, remain. They are the bedrock of the college. They are your most effective messenger.

Your job is to so inspire them with your spirit and vision, commitment and promise— that your message and theirs is locked in a warm embrace.

58. You are not the chief academic officer. It can easily happen that you end up spending an inordinate amount of time in academic affairs. You can easily slip into this activity especially if you have been a chief academic officer in the past.

This isn't how you should be spending your time. You need to make a change if you don't have a superb academic officer in place.

As one president put it to me, "The new president should probably be spending more time at the country club romancing a donor than in the faculty dining room."

59. Go to them. When meeting with faculty and senior staff, it's a good idea to visit them in their office instead of having them come to yours. It provides a great opportunity to get a feeling for their environment and the kind of office they maintain. The piles on their desk, the books on their shelf, and whether it's the sort of spot a student might enjoy visiting.

Going to their office also provides you with a comfortable and quick exit plan. You simply thank the person for the visit and leave. You don't have to worry about your Assistant poking her head in the door to tell you that your new appointment has arrived. (Even though there may not be a new appointment!)

60. Welcome the malcontent. You need to be a friend and supporter of new ideas. That goes for faculty, senior staff, and board members, too. The disgruntled person can easily be an irritant to you. You sometimes seek what Bob Dylan once called, "shelter from the storm."

Just remember that the seeds of progress are often rooted in the disgruntled and unhappy person. As the saying goes, "When the tide goes out, the rocks begin to show." It's often the pebble in the shoe that causes you to take appropriate notice and action.

61. Incite change. Create an environment where change is embraced. That is true even if you inherit a welcoming culture and a college that is doing exceedingly well.

Change is inevitable. In fact, it may have been the major reason you were hired. If the college is standing still, you are on the losing side. The parade will pass you by. In today's world, you can't stand still.

62. You need to do a better job of marketing. Young men and women who consider you for entrance are smarter, more selective, and more demanding than ever before. They have higher expectations for academic quality, extra activities, and overall performance. And good grief— they want it all at a lower cost. You will have to do much more than ever before in attracting them to your campus.

Some colleges are totally uninteresting— like the creamy surface of a yogurt cup before you dig in. There needs to be *buzz* on your campus. And you are in charge of the *buzz*. It doesn't just happen. You create it.

You need not be the idea person. Others can do that. You nurture an environment for exciting new things to happen. You're the one who lights the match to the fireworks.

63. Change is not popular. You may not win any popularity contests when you make decisions for change. If you believe that everyone will find your changes desirable— then, as the song goes, "I've been looking for love in all the wrong places."

There are those who will want to hold on to what they believe is the golden past. There will be the naysayers and the hand-wringers who tell you that the changes you plan can't be done. You may feel like you are walking through mud.

But persevere. St. Basil said: "No one who shuns the blows and the dust of battle wins a crown." Make the necessary changes. That is why you were brought to the college.

64. Even when things are going exceedingly well, be wary. Be vigilant. In every cycle of success, there comes a time when you need to look very carefully at what is happening. You can't afford to coast. The time to institute new and exciting programs, create exceptional new possibilities, dream great dreams— is when you are most successful.

65. Honor the past but look to the future. Pay tribute and honor to past achievements of the college, and glorify the traditions. But make it clear you look to the future for the college's greatest accomplishments.

You have a disquieting distaste for the hoary past. You are vigilantly open and aggressively attuned to the future. The play is ready to begin— and you have the major role. You seek change and welcome it with open arms.

66. Aim for the very top. There's plenty of room at the bottom. Your objective for the college is to be the very best it can possibly be. You will settle for nothing less. Your credo is to be unexcelled. It's the hymn you sing. You will tolerate nothing less.

67. You become a leader. True leadership exists when your staff and faculty follow when they have the freedom not to. You are not leading if they follow because they have no choice. If you hold a gun to someone's head, they will do what you tell them to. But that's not leadership.

68. You inspire. You do not manage the operation. You lead the college. There is a great distinction. A manager operates from the top down. Managers *push* people. As a leader, you *pull* people up. If you do not provide leadership, the college falters.

69. The key to leadership. Managing is the *science* of getting other people to do things that need to be done at the college. Leadership is the *art* of inspiring them to do that. That's your job. You are the leader.

70. Make dreams come true. Your job, as the college president and its leader, is to make individual dreams come true. You help your faculty and staff reach their highest aspirations. This is in exchange for the staff and faculty helping make the dreams of the college come true.

71. Energy is important. For the president, high energy is essential. Everyone can feel the rumble and roar. It's contagious. If you have energy, it shows. Even on a day when you don't feel the whir and whiz, you have to display it. People expect it from their leader.

You will have more energy if you are physically fit. You will look better and feel better. You somehow have more self-assurance.

When you are fatigued, your resistance is lowered. You make poor decisions. You can't handle stress. Being an effective president takes energy, and that means being physically and emotionally fit.

72. Be curious. Curiosity is a prime attribute of the successful president. The more they know, the more they seem to want to know. You are always probing, searching, exploring. You understand that the greatest lesson of all is that there is always more to learn, always more to find out.

You can identify with Einstein. He said: "I don't believe I have any special talents. I am only passionately, insatiably curious."

73. Teach and sell. You inspire others to dream more, do more, and become more. You are inspiring, selling, giving hope. If you're not doing that, you are not leading.

74. Integrity is everything. Having the proper character and integrity isn't important. It is everything. In a recent *Fortune Magazine* article of the nation's greatest leaders, the giants—integrity leads the list of the most important attributes. It is the first law of the college president. If you don't believe the messenger, you won't believe the message.

I was in a classroom at Exeter Academy when the teacher was stressing to the students seated around the Harkness Table the importance of gaining trust. One young man asked how it was possible to win trust. The teacher looked over the glasses tilted on the edge of his nose, and said dryly: "Try being trustworthy."

75. Deliver on your word. Do what you say you will do. That is the Gospel of leadership. You must know who you are, say who you are, and then do what you say.

Did you skip lightly over that. I'll repeat for emphasis because it's so important. Know who you are. Say who you are. Do what you say.

76. It's not about you. It's essential you keep in mind that your role at the college is really not about you. It's about the students. That's what it's all about. Most successful presidents have a rather healthy ego. It takes that. But being a leader takes some humility, also. You were not anointed. You were appointed.

77. You must listen. One of the most important attributes of a strong president is the ability to listen. You listen. Listen. Listen. Hearing and listening are not synonymous— they are distinctly different. Active listening is one of the most important aspects of your job.

78. Don't listen to respond. It's important to know that you don't listen in order to respond. What? No, you listen to get information.

You become addicted. You listen to everything that is going on— the students, the faculty, the staff, the board. You listen. It is the only way to gain new information and insights. If you don't listen actively, you're not getting all the information you need.

79. Help others. Your job as president is to help others stand on tiptoes. Your greatest achievement is to endow staff and faculty (and trustees, too) to reach their highest aspirations. That's what it is all about. You are the president, and you empower all around you.

80. Keep an eye on the competition. There are other colleges competing for your students, faculty members, staff, and donors. Keep an eye on what other colleges are doing and make certain you are leading the parade. Infinite vigilance is the price of being the greatest, the fastest, and the most exciting.

81. Things may go awry. Just when you think you may be on the right track, the needle skittles. There are times when things don't work out as planned. This is what Jim Harrison refers to when he says that life is a near-death experience.

The problems often happen when the new president does not make the staff changes that are needed, does not execute effectively, is not willing to hear bad news when necessary, is unwilling to make decisions, and doesn't take proper care of the staff.

This won't happen to you. You know better!

82. Personal skills are essential. A college community can overlook a great deal if the president has skill in working with people. Your job is not necessarily to win a popularity contest—although you likely will. Your responsibility is to engender confidence, inspire people, give hope, be a good listener, and be empathetic. If you do all of this, you will have good personal relations.

83. It takes time. Before you become too pleased with your progress, here's something to keep in mind. You cannot be considered an unmitigated success until your appointment is unanimously ratified in the minds and hearts of the board— two years from the time of your appointment.

84. It was ordained. For many presidents, there is a strong sense that you were destined to lead the college at this time in its history. It was fate. You are marked for greatness and it was intended that you bring the college to its highest level of achievement in its history.

85. Have fun. The work is arduous, the hours are long, the challenges multiply faster than imaginable. There is always, as they say, more than you can say grace over. Pope John Paul could have been talking directly to you when he said: "Life is precious. Love it. Use it. Pour yourself into it. Spend yourself."

The job is exhilarating. It's not even work to you— it's fun. It's a great joy. You are at life's epicenter. Live all you can. It's a grievous mistake not to.

"He who is inclined to making many pronouncements and practicing profundity, is in grave danger of being compared to the blacksmith's bellows— providing great bursts of hot air under pressure, but having not spark nor fire in itself."

– John Lewis Russell

16

OH...AND ONE THING MORE
(The Afterword)

There is no particular rationale to the presidents I chose to visit with. They are simply men and women I work with or know well. Those I respect greatly.

The institutions they head come in all sizes and shapes. From Oxford University (UK) and the University of Illinois to Thomas Aquinas College with 400 students.

Of particular interest to me is the commonality of the issues and problems ("challenges," as Joe White prefers). But what stands out most of all is the critical importance of the first 120 days in office. That refrain was the same from everyone. Everyone!

"I'm absolutely convinced," says Jake Schrum, "the course of the presidency is set in the first 120 days." Steve Jenning agrees: "The premise is exactly right. It's the crucial time." Joe White is emphatic: "In those first 120 days, it is determined whether you will have a successful tenure or not."

I have unbounded respect when I read some of the inspirational titles of a few of the classics in our field. *The Entrepreneurial President,* for instance, by James Fisher or *The Landmark, The Uses of the University* by Clark Kerr, former president of the University of California. *Beyond the Ivory Tower,* by former Harvard president Derek Bok.

Those titles alone create a certain reverence, mentioned only in hushed and whispered words— much like an acolyte speaking to the Papal Father. These are the kinds of books you would like to have in a prominent place on your book shelf or be seen reading on your next airplane trip.

Very impressive. ("I couldn't help noticing what you're reading. Are you involved in college or university work? Oh really, a college president. Oh, how interesting . . .")

I recognize that my book is a bit of what you would call, *nuts and bolts*. There's not much philosophy. Philosophy was not my intention. I won't be offended if you do not keep the book on the edge of your desk for all to see.

You have perhaps heard the story about the earnest young missionary who talked non-stop with cannibals for three full days. They seemed to listen with great respect. Then they said grace and put him in a big pot with boiling water over his head. They cooked and ate him. The purpose of this book is to make certain you don't get into hot water and get cooked.

I did want to provide a guideline, a working manual of sorts. I sought to help a new president get off to a running start. If I achieve that, it will be thanks sufficient. jp

APPENDIX*

LEADERSHIP INVENTORY

STATEMENT OF UNDERSTANDING

101 ATTRIBUTES AND CHARACTERISTICS OF A LEADER

* All items in the Appendix may be copied without permission. Attribution will be appreciated. Visit my website at www. jeroldpanas.com for a full size copy (pdf) of these documents.

LEADERSHIP INVENTORY

I have developed a Leadership Inventory. The one you see here was designed specifically for the college president.

I want you to review it. But instead of marking up your book, e-mail me for as many copies as you would like (ideas@jeroldpanas.com).

Here is how I would like you to use it. Take the test. Go ahead. Take it! Be harshly objective.

I have taken it myself. It can severely test one's ego.

Take the test. Then select someone from your senior staff who will fill it out herself. Next, ask her to have each one of your senior staff fill out the form and send it to her. It's important that it not be signed or identified.

Have her average all of the scores including her own. And then, have her send the averaged returns to you.

I've gone through the exercise myself. In my case, I had our senior person in the firm review the Inventory individually with our five vice presidents. Each person, one-on-one, each item. All were promised anonymity.

In some cases, they discussed a specific item at some length in order to get a proper assessment. All of the ratings from the staff were totaled and then averaged. I received a copy of the average.

I took every item with a score of four (there weren't a good many below that) and made those items a matter of staff discussion. The discussion was extremely helpful.

I have field-tested the Leadership Inventory. I am convinced that the scores and the evaluations are on target. Some of the questions, by the way, may seem redundant. But there are certain shadings of a question that I feel are important. jp

LEADERSHIP INVENTORY

Rate yourself on a five-point scale— "five" (5) being *highly effective* to "one" (1) being *highly ineffective*. If you wish, have someone else evaluate you in the second column.

5	*Highly Effective*
4	*Effective*
3	*Somewhat Effective*
2	*Not Very Effective*
1	*Not Effective*

Consider your own or your colleague's effectiveness in the areas that follow. How satisfied are you with the way he or she (or you) . . .

Building Partnerships	Your Rating	Another's Rating
1. Embraces the value of diversity within the entire college* community (including culture, race, sex, or age for students, senior staff, faculty, and employees).		
2. Does not feel challenged by an effective senior staff** or staff member.		
3. Treats staff as partners and valued colleagues.		
4. Has the ability to motivate staff and faculty.		
5. Keeps a riveting focus on the priorities of the college.		
6. Unites the staff of the college into an effective team.		
7. Develops a powerful *espirit de corps* throughout the staff and faculty.		
8. Is not negative or critical about a person in front of staff.		
9. Discourages destructive comments from staff about other people or groups in the college.		
10. Builds effective collaboration with other organizations and colleges.		
11. Creates a network of relationships with the staff that helps to get things done.		
TOTAL:		

* Throughout the Inventory, "college" refers to both colleges and universities
** Throughout the Inventory, "staff" refers mostly to senior staff

Sharing Leadership	Your Rating	Another's Rating
12. Willingly shares leadership with co-workers and colleagues.		
13. Encourages staff members to grow personally and professionally.		
14. Defers to others when they have more expertise.		
15. With others, strives to arrive at satisfactory outcomes.		
16. Creates an environment where people focus on the larger good of the college.		
17. Doesn't get bogged down in details.		
18. Doesn't have to be hands-on for all that is going on.		
TOTAL:		

Creating a Shared Vision	Your Rating	Another's Rating
19. Creates and communicates a clear vision for the college.		
20. Effectively involves appropriate people in decision making.		
21. Inspires staff to work together to achieve a common vision.		
22. Develops an effective strategy to achieve the college's vision.		
23. Clearly identifies priorities for the college.		
24. Encourages long range strategic planning.		
TOTAL:		

Developing People	Your Rating	Another's Rating
25. Strives for excellence in his or her personal performance and that of the staff.		
26. Consistently treats all people with dignity.		
27. Asks staff what they need to do their work better.		
28. Provides staff what they need to do their work better.		
29. Ensures that people receive the training they need to succeed.		
30. Is an effective coach for the staff.		
31. Provides professional development feedback and evaluation in a timely manner.		
32. Provides effective recognition for the achievement of others.		
33. Not satisfied with mediocre work.		
34. Demanding but not unrealistic or unreasonable.		
35. Accessible and approachable.		
TOTAL:		

Empowering People	Your Rating	Another's Rating
36. Has a demeanor that inspires others.		
37. Builds confidence in staff members.		
38. Understands and demonstrates that the staff and faculty are the most important resource in the college.		
39. Takes risks in letting others make decisions.		

40. Provides rewards for doing a good job.		
41. Gives people the freedom they need to do their job well.		
42. Hires staff who have strengths that he or she does not possess.		
43. Trusts people enough to let go (avoids micromanagement). Delegates freely.		
44. Provides public recognition for work well done.		
45. Demonsrates confidence in the staff.		
46. Helps staff and faculty reach their highest aspirations.		
TOTAL:		

Achieving Personal Mastery	Your Rating	Another's Rating
47. Reads for professional growth.		
48. Understands his or her own strengths and weaknesses.		
49. Maintains a positive attitude even in difficult times.		
50. Invests in ongoing personal development.		
51. Willing to share the credit.		
52. Good at "reading" people.		
53. Demonstrates effective emotional responses in a variety of situations.		
54. Is decisive in making decisions.		
55. Willing to make tough decisions and take the responsibility.		

	Your Rating	Another's Rating
56. Has an intuitive "feel" for making the right decisions.		
57. Willing to take the responsibility for a poor decision.		
58. Lives a balanced life: family, work, and play.		
59. Demonstrates self-confidence as the president and the leader. Self-assured, but not cocky.		
60. Has an ability to focus on the task at hand.		
61. Is willing to say "no" when necessary.		
62. Displays high level of energy.		
63. Displays a passion and commitment for the college and its mission.		
64. Has a presence that "fills a room".		
TOTAL:		

Encouraging Constructive Dialogue	Your Rating	Another's Rating
65. Asks staff what he or she can do personally to improve.		
66. Listens to others.		
67. Accepts constructive feedback in a positive manner— not defensive.		
68. Strives to understand the other person's frame of reference.		
69. Encourages staff to challenge the *status quo*.		
TOTAL:		

Demonstrates Integrity	Your Rating	Another's Rating
70. Exemplifies integrity at all times in personal and professional life— through honesty, consistency, reliability, and discretion.		
71. Ensures that the highest standards for ethical behavior are practiced throughout the college.		
72. Avoids self-serving behavior.		
73. Courageously stands up for what he or she believes in.		
74. Is a role model for living the college's values.		
75. Leads by example.		
TOTAL:		

Leading Change	Your Rating	Another's Rating
76. Sees change as an opportunity, not a problem.		
77. Challenges the system when change is needed.		
78. Accepts new ideas from others.		
79. Embraces the latest of technology in the college to help increase productivity and effectiveness.		
80. Thrives in ambiguous situations.		
81. Is a creative person.		
82. Encourages creativity and innovation in others.		
83. Effectively transforms creative ideas into highly productive results for the college.		

84. Demonstrates flexibility.		
85. Willing to challenge the *status quo* and old culture of the college.		
TOTAL:		

Anticipates Opportunities	Your Rating	Another's Rating
86. Invests in learning about future trends.		
87. Effectively anticipates future opportunities.		
88. Inspires people to focus on future opportunities— not just tactical objectives.		
89. Develops ideas to meet the needs of the a new environment and changing times.		
90. Makes certain the college is vital and progressive.		
TOTAL:		

Ensuring Constituency Satisfaction	Your Rating	Another's Rating
91. Inspires the staff to achieve high levels of satisfaction among the entire college community.		
92. Looks at everything from the ultimate perspective of the college community.		
93. Regularly solicits input from all segments of the college community.		
94. Consistently delivers on commitments to the college community.		
95. Understands the many options available to his or her constituencies and how this affects the college.		
TOTAL:		

Maintaining a Competitive Advantage	Your Rating	Another's Rating
96. Communicates a positive, "can do" sense or urgency toward getting a job done.		
97. Holds staff accountable for their results.		
98. Successfully elimnates waste and unneeded costs without compromising the college's effectiveness.		
99. Provides products and services that help the college have a clear competitive advantage.		
100. Achieves results that lead to long term success.		
TOTAL:		
GRAND TOTAL:		

KEY TO EVALUATION

Review the ratings in each Section. Determine where improvement may be necessary. Then total your entire score.

401 to 500	You are a highly effective president. The college is indeed fortunate to have you heading the operation.
301 to 400	You are quite effective. Work on those characteristics that need improvement.
201 to 300	You require improvement. Perhaps having a mentor or coach will be helpful. If you are intent on improvement, dedicate yourself to reading on the topic, attend relevant seminars, and seek counsel from others.
Below 200	You may be in the wrong slot. Perhaps another position, (one of importance but not leadership) may provie you with more fulfillment. Afterall, it should be fun.

STATEMENT OF UNDERSTANDING

STATEMENT OF UNDERSTANDING
FOR MEMBERS OF THE
BOARD OF TRUSTEES

As a member of the Board of Trustees of Thomas Aquinas College, I am fully committed to the vision and work of the College and am dedicated to carrying out its mission. I understand that in accepting this position on the Board:

1   One of my most important responsibilities, with other Board members, is the hiring and on-going evaluation of the President. I shall do everything possible to support the work of the President, but shall not become involved in the management of the College. If the work of the President is not up to agreed upon standards, it is my responsibility, with other Board members, to take whatever action is appropriate.

2   In addition to being committed to the vision of the College and its mission, I understand that it is my duty to make certain that we have the necessary funds to meet our mission— "No funds, no mission..."

3   I shall do all I can to support the staff, and encourage them to grow professionally and personally. I will be prepared to assist them whenever it is appropriate.

    I also understand that there are times I must stay out of their way! I won't manage—but I will encourage and expect the best results possible, the highest quality work possible, and ever-increasing production. Working together with the staff, we can attain high objectives, and ultimately achieve the mission and vision of Thomas Aquinas College.

4   With other Board members, I am responsible for friendraising and fundraising for the College. I will work with other board members in developing our dreams and high expectations for the future, and will take an active part in reviewing, approving, monitoring, and achieving these objectives.

5   I take a responsibility to know as much as I can about the College—its work and outreach, and its vision for the future.

6   I shall give, what is for me, as substantial a financial donation as possible to the College. I may give this as a one-time donation each year, or I may commit to give a certain amount several times during the year.

7   I understand that as a Board member, I lead the way. I am a model for others to follow. If I, as a Board member, do not care enough to work and give, why should anyone else?

8   I will actively engage in fundraising in whatever ways are best suited for me and most effectively serve the purposes of Thomas Aquinas. These may include individual solicitation, undertaking special events, writing mail appeals, and the like. I am willing to make this good-faith agreement to do my best and to raise as much money as I can.

9   I will be an enthusiastic booster, a positive advocate for Thomas Aquinas College.

10 I shall attend Board meetings and be available for phone consultation. If I am not able to meet my obligations as a Board member, I understand that I may be asked to offer my resignation.

11 I recognize that I am to provide for the future by offering studied input in the strategic planning process. I shall help decide which goals should receive priority and help determine how these are to be financed.

12 I shall evaluate the progress and results of the College by asking appropriate and searching questions: Are we doing as well as we should? Are we meeting our goals and objectives? Are we serving students to optimum levels? If not, why not? Are we getting better and better results as time goes on?

13 I shall join and become active on at least one Board Committee.

14 I shall bring the **six A**s to my Board tenure. I shall:

   be an **Ambassador**—*to help tell our story*
   be an **Advisor**—*and make effective decisions on policy and programs*
   be an **Advocate**—*be a roaring enthusiast for the cause of the College*
   provide **Access**—*help bring and influence others on behalf of our mission*
   provide **Affluence**—*give as much as I possibly can*
   provide **Assistance**—*volunteer for as many activities as possible*

15 Among the Boards I serve on, I shall consider my work with Thomas Aquinas Collge to be my most important priority—or at the very least, no lower than my second interest.

16 In signing this document, I understand that no quotas are being set, and no rigid standards of measurement and achievement are being established. Every Board member makes a statement of faith to be a partner with every other Board member to strive for the success of our great cause. We trust each other to carry out the above agreements to the best of our ability.

(Signature) _____
               Board Member

IN RETURN,
THOMAS AQUINAS COLLEGE IS RESPONSIBLE TO YOU
IN A NUMBER OF WAYS.
HERE ARE SOME:

1   *To use your time in the most effective way possible so that your involvement and service to Thomas Aquinas is of consequence.*

2   *You will regularly receive status reports and information about our work, service, and progress.*

3   *You can call on the us, the Chair and President, and the senior staff at any time to discuss programs, policies, goals, and objectives.*

4   *You can count on me, as president, and the staff to support your work in every way possible.*

5   *We shall do our best to make Board meetings meaningful and productive, with as little lost and meaningless time as possible.*

6   *We shall encourage you to take an increasingly larger role in leadership.*

7   *Board members and staff will respond to the best of their ability in a straightforward and thorough fashion to any questions you have that you feel are necessary to carry out your responsibilities to the College.*

8   *You can expect the staff and all Board members to make this the most rewarding and fulfilling experience you have ever had.*

(Signature) _____
                        Chair of the Board

(Signature) _____
                        President

101 ATTRIBUTES AND CHARACTERISTICS OF A LEADER

I have put together a list of 101 attributes and characteristics of a leader. Go ahead— just try to add anything! If you come-up with something I've left out, e-mail me with your addition (ideas@jeroldpanas.com). In the next edition for the book, I'll include yours— and give you credit.

By the way, don't be concerned if you don't have all the 101 traits. You are still going to be an outstanding president.

1. Accommodates different viewpoints
2. Acknowledges personal deficiencies
3. Adaptability
4. Admits mistakes
5. Ambitious
6. Analytical thinker
7. Appreciates art and music
8. Believes the best in others
9. Brings out the best in others
10. Calm under fire
11. Capitalizes on personal assets
12. Caring
13. Civility
14. Collaborative
15. Commitment
16. Communication skills
17. Compassion
18. Confident
19. Consensus builder
20. Continuous learner
21. Cooperativeness
22. Courtesy
23. Creative
24. Decision making skills
25. Dependability
26. Determination
27. Devoid of prejudice
28. Discipline
29. Driven to excellence
30. Empathy
31. Energetic
32. Engages others
33. Enjoys life
34. Enthusiasm
35. Fairness
36. Faithfulness

37. Finds work fulfilling
38. Flexibility
39. Forgiving
40. Friendliness
41. Future thinking
42. Generosity
43. Genuineness
44. Gracious
45. Happy
46. Healthy
47. Helps others develop
48. Honesty
49. Hopefulness
50. Independent thinker
51. Influences others
    by example
52. Ingenuity
53. Initiative
54. Insightful
55. Inspiring
56. Integrity
57. Intelligence
58. Intuitive
59. Invites input from others
60. Keeps focused
61. Kind
62. Leadership
63. Learns from errors
64. Listening
65. Loves and is loved
66. Loyalty
67. Manages conflict and stress
68. Modest
69. Optimism
70. Patience

71. Patriotism
72. Perceptive
73. Perseverance
74. Philanthropic
75. Polite
76. Positive Attitude
77. Prayer
78. Punctual
79. Reads
80. Resourceful
81. Respect for others
82. Responsibility
83. Self-sufficient
84. Self-control
85. Sense of humor
86. Service to others
87. Sharing
88. Social skills
89. Spontaneity
90. Strong belief system
91. Takes time to volunteer
92. Tenacious
93. Thinks out of the box
94. Tolerance
95. Trust in others
96. Trustworthiness
97. Visionary
98. Welcomes change
99. Willing to dare
100. Winning others over
101. Work ethic